A Woman's Place…
The Crucial Roles of Women in Family Business

Ann M. Dugan, Sharon P. Krone,
Kelly LeCouvie, Ph.D.,
Jennifer M. Pendergast, Ph.D.,
Denise H. Kenyon-Rouvinez, Ph.D.,
and Amy M. Schuman

The Family Business Consulting Group, Inc.®
1220-B Kennestone Circle
Marietta, GA 30066
888-421-0110
www.efamilybusiness.com

ISBN: 1-891652-21-4

A Woman's Place...
The Crucial Roles of Women in Family Business

A woman of valour who can find? for her price is far above rubies.

Proverbs 31:10

Contents

Exhibits

I.
Introduction: Family Firms on the Brink of Opportunity

Girls can do anything.
—Popular slogan

Early in 2006, an article on succession in family-owned independent bookstores appeared in *Publishers Weekly* magazine. It's unlikely the article or anything like it would have appeared 25 years before. Five businesses were included in the piece and women had a significant role in every one of them. The two most famous stores—the Strand Book Store in New York City and Powell's Books in Portland, Oregon—were both run by men but daughters had been designated as their successors. Two were operated by male-female partners (one a married couple), and the fifth, Bunch of Grapes Bookstore in Vineyard Haven, Massachusetts, was owned by Ann Nelson, whose son, Jon, a former Black Hawk pilot, joined the business in 2002.[1] Lest you think a book store is inconsequential, Strand, an 80-year-old family business, employs 200 people, and Powell's provides nearly 500 jobs.

In many ways, the *Publisher's Weekly* article epitomizes the rapid changes that family firms are experiencing. While family businesses are still primarily a male domain, more women are running family businesses than ever before, and more aspire to leadership. Many women who decide not to work in the family firm are nevertheless assuming other roles that support the business, such as board chair or family council president. In the United States, parents increasingly choose to pass shares of their family businesses to all their children equally instead of following the ancient tradition of primogeniture—leaving the business to the first-born son. As a result, record numbers of women are becoming shareholders in their family's firms.

These changes signal that family businesses are on the brink of a new and potentially wonderful opportunity. Family-owned companies benefit enormously when they open themselves up to 100 percent of the talent pool that's available in their families, not just the traditional 50 or so percent – the males in the family. By welcoming all who can make a contribution, business-owning families stand to increase their competitiveness, their staying power, their capacity to grow and their ability to succeed in handing the business to the next generation.

We are seeing changes in all sectors of family business. Women are leaders of or playing other significant roles in family companies that range from cosmetics to meat packing, from construction to textiles manufacturing, from finance to sheet-metal fabrication and from automobile sales to travel and entertainment. Women, it appears, know no bounds. And recent research suggests that women-owned family businesses have a higher rate of productivity than those owned by men.

We have struggled with the question of who this book is for. Should it be for the women in family businesses themselves? Should it be aimed particularly at young women who dream of running the company? Should it be focused on the family members and others surrounding such ambitious, talented women, helping these people understand and accept the change that is inevitable and showing them how they can help women succeed in their families' companies?

We recognized, however, that women play a multitude of roles, and some of their most significant contributions are made not inside the business but in the family. Instead of taking an "either-or" approach, we offer this book to both the women themselves, whatever role they choose to play, and to all the people around them, who can help pave the way for women's success and, in so doing, support the continuity of their family businesses. This broader approach respects the notion that just as males can't make a contribution to a family business unless they are brought up in an environment that supports their development and their success, neither can females.

Whatever category best describes you, the reader, here is what we think you can gain from this book:

1. Women in business-owning families. We will be exploring a variety of roles, including: those who set their sights on holding senior leadership positions in family businesses or who already hold such posts, women married to founders/CEOs, widows of founders/CEOs, women who marry into family businesses, women shareholders who are or are not working in the business, girls and young women who will be future shareholders, and women who aspire to or already hold leadership positions in their families.

Women will find suggestions for how to prepare themselves for and be effective in whatever roles they choose. They will gain ideas from other women on how to meet the challenge of work/life balance, manage stress, and sharpen their financial skills, as well as how to work with advisors and other key non-family figures.

You may wonder why we have chosen to focus on women. Is preparing women to be effective in their chosen roles different than the preparation for men? You will find that some of the information in this book is valuable regardless of gender, but we have chosen to focus on women because they have been traditionally overlooked for leadership roles in business and therefore face some unique challenges in preparing themselves.

If you are a woman already in a significant leadership role in the business or the family, you no doubt already "get it." This book then is not so much for you as it is for those around you. Nevertheless, you might take pleasure in discovering thàt there are others who understand you and who share similar experiences.

We believe that what you read in these pages will deepen your understanding of and appreciation for the contributions that you and other women are already making to your family business or inspire you to aim for roles that you had not even imagined before.

2. Business-owning families. If you are part of a business-owning family, you will find guidance not only on preparing daughters and nieces for business participation but also on readying the whole family for the inclusion of women in the business—possibly at the highest levels. You will learn how to encourage and support women family members and value what they have to offer a family firm and the family that owns it.

You will also have a chance to explore thoughts about raising girls and young women to become financially knowledgeable, as well as about educating them to be effective shareholders of the family company.

3. Spouses of successful women—women of wealth or women in key positions in their families' companies. Life partners or potential life partners of successful women in business-owning families will find this book useful in understanding not only the challenges the women face but also their own importance in supporting a family business by supporting their wives or significant others. This book offers some guidance in managing and enjoying relationships with accomplished, high-profile women, as well as suggests what successful women think it takes to partner with women like themselves.

Husbands in more traditional relationships—perhaps older husbands who have not shared financial information with their spouses in the past—will gain insight into why their wives (and perhaps their daughters) need to know more about family and business finances and what they need to know.

4. The "outsiders." These are individuals outside the family who work with the business or family in a professional capacity and who exercise a great deal of influence on both. They include non-family executives, independent board members, advisors (such as attorneys, accountants and bankers), and stakeholders (suppliers, customers and franchisors). If you are an outsider, expect to gain greater knowledge about how to work successfully with or in a family business where women are encouraged to rise to their full potential.

In Chapter II, "Farewell, Primogeniture!," we look at the evolution of family businesses with respect to women. We report on some of the available research and combine what it shows with our own observations.

As pleased and excited as we are that more and more women are running family firms and doing so with great skill and self-assurance, we recognize that women play all kinds of roles that support the success of a family business and often are essential to it. Chapter III, "How Women Contribute," describes many of these roles and is, in a number of respects, the heart of this book. Some of women's roles have been or still are invisible or unrecognized or simply behind the scenes. We see the role of "mother" as critical to family business, as do some of the most professionally successful women you will meet in this book. We have a deep respect for the contributions that women make, but our research for this chapter led us to an even greater admiration for and expanded understanding of what women do for family firms than we had before.

A thought about daughter-in-laws. With some frequency, families have felt threatened by in-laws, fearing that a divorce would lead to an in-law gaining control of some of the shares of the business and having a destructive impact on the company. We have been impressed, however, by the many stories of passionately loyal and intelligent daughters-in-law who have given a family business new life or who have preserved it for the next generation. You will be introduced to some of these in-laws in Chapter III and throughout the book.

Chapter III also offers insights into how women have prepared themselves for some of the responsibilities they have taken on and how you, too, can prepare for the role you want to play.

Chapter IV, "Finding the Right Balance: Work and Life," addresses the never-ending dilemma of trying to give sufficient attention to both work and personal/family needs. Examples of what other women and their families do to meet this challenge will provide comfort to you in your own struggle with work/life balance issues as well as offer ideas for moving forward.

Couples buck tradition when the woman earns more or is perceived as the more successful of the pair or where, because of family wealth, a woman brings more assets to the relationship than her life partner does. Chapter V, "The Challenge to Couples," looks at such situations and offers thoughts on ways to deal with a new reality in which wives often out-earn husbands.

It's easy to assume that women from family businesses might have more understanding of financial issues than other women do, but, unfortunately, our experience tells us that this is not necessarily so. Chapter VI, "Becoming Financially Literate," helps women and their significant others understand what women in business-owning families need to know about finances. It also provides guidance to a woman on whether or not to assume leadership of the family business if her husband/CEO unexpectedly passes away.

Chapter VII, "Working with 'Outsiders,'" considers an important segment of a woman's environment: the non-family figures in her life. They can be supporters or self-serving exploiters, mentors or withholders of information. They can make major contributions to helping a woman achieve her goals, or they can undermine her self-confidence and attempt to dominate her. A woman needs to understand these differences and family outsiders need to understand what the woman's perspective is. This chapter will help.

Chapter I

"Women, Communication and Leadership," Chapter VIII, offers insight into two topics where popular current thought says women are different from men: communication and leadership. We look at some of those differences but more important, we offer some pragmatic suggestions. When it comes to communication, the point is that women and men need to be communicated with equally and have an equal chance to be heard and understood. When it comes to leadership, one should be skilled in several styles, whether you're male or female, and to use the appropriate style for a given situation.

Our final chapter, Chapter IX, "What Else Women and Families Can Do," challenges some remaining assumptions that readers might still have about women in family business. It also offers new and useful ways to think about gender and family firms.

Where appropriate, many chapters offer special sections with guidelines that women, their partners, their families and the family "outsiders" will find of use. At the end of the book, you will also find a list of resources, such as readings that can offer you further knowledge or organizations that can provide you with specific kinds of help.

Many chapters are enhanced by the stories of women in family-owned businesses who agreed to be interviewed for this book. They are Martha Jahn Martin, Angela G. Santerini, Emily Heisley Stoeckel, Marcy Syms, Nancy F. Waichler, and Georgia Berner.

You will discover that this book is told primarily from a woman's point of view. The authors are women. The interviewees are women. The stories that are told are generally stories about women. We felt that it was important that this be a book in which women were heard—particularly since women are now being listened to and valued on a conscious level in their family businesses and allowed to make contributions that are both visible and recognized.

Research on women in family business is still sparse and we will share with you some of what is available. However, this book is based not only on research and interviews with women, it is also built on our combined professional experience, which exceeds 85 years of family business consulting and academic work and employment in family firms. In addition to our current professions, five of the six of us have a personal connection with a family business:

Kelly LeCouvie is active in her family's 50-year-old transportation company in an advisory capacity and as a part of its senior management team. Her participation has enabled her to experience the joy of family members working together, and the challenges of managing through conflict, succession planning, and setting strategic direction for the organization. She works with her mother, a co-founder of the business, as well as with three of her brothers. "The business was always a dinner-table topic in our home," Kelly recalls. "Despite my having four brothers, I was never deterred from working in the business, and did on and off when I was a student." Today, she observes, the third-generation girls work part-time right alongside the third-generation boys.

While Denise H. Kenyon-Rouvinez doesn't come directly from a business-owning family, she virtually grew up in one. In the 1950s, her grandparents and aunt and uncle started a wine-making company that is today Switzerland's third largest wine producer. The twenty-five cousins of Denise's generation were all expected to work in the company in the summer and on Saturdays. They spent time in the vineyards and, as Denise recalls, their grandparents patiently taught them, at a very early age, how to carefully pick the grapes, how to manually label the wine bottles and how to be polite around clients. The wine company was where she first learned to work and, she says, it provided "great lessons for the rest of my life."

To this day, it rankles Amy M. Schuman that her family never considered inviting her or her sister because they were female to explore joining the family's electrical contracting business. "And truthfully," Amy recalls, "I showed no interest." Even though he had no interest either, her younger brother was encouraged to join the company. He pursued a career in advertising instead. Amy's brother-in-law did join the family firm but, eventually, it went bankrupt. "Now, here I am, helping other businesses but I couldn't help my own," Amy says. "I do wonder if I could have helped make it a success if I had been a part of things. I need to blame myself as much as the grown-ups around me for not perceiving the opportunity and taking hold of it."

Ann M. Dugan comes from a Brunswick, Georgia, business-owning family that has supplied most of the lumber and building materials that went into homes, resorts, and businesses on Georgia's Sea Island, St. Simon's Island and Jekyll Island. "The ownership of the business was always passed down through the men in my family, but many of the women were very instrumental behind the scenes and critical to the fact that the business is now in its fifth generation and going strong," says Ann. From the business and her extended family, Ann learned the responsibility that a well-known business-owning family carries in a small community. Her grandfather was a long-time mayor and other family members were community leaders for many years. Ann is also the founder of two successful start-up ventures now operated by family members.

Sharon P. Krone was aware that her extended family was active in their family business when she was growing up. "I now know what a delicate transition they endured from the previous generation—with its share of conflict and strained relationships, but what has given the company strength and staying power into the future is their openness to both male and female leadership and a place for everyone who has interest in being a part of it."

Both of Sharon's in-laws came from family businesses and she was "fortunate to see family values, including the value of women's contributions, incorporated in these families." Sharon was drawn to family business as a professional focus after coming across the work of John L. Ward, a leader in the field. In 1994, as a research fellow under Ward's tutelage, she founded the Family Business Communications Institute at the Loyola University Chicago Family Business Center. "It was an effort to design a curriculum to teach families how to facilitate their own family meetings," she says. I was very intensely involved in 'What are families doing with their family meetings? What are the successful stories? What were the crash-and-burn stories? How could a facilitator help? How do we train a family member to be a neutral party in that process?'"

Jennifer M. Pendergast is the only one of us who does not come from a family business or has not had one in the family or ever worked in one, but she shares our passion for family firms. "My interest came from a background in corporate governance and the unique governance challenges faced by family businesses," she says. An authority on business strategy, she adds, "I was drawn to the ways that family businesses can use their advantages—knowledge of the business, long-term perspective, and business culture—to develop successful strategies."

We all love and are committed to family businesses, and we are equally committed to the full participation of women family members in those businesses, according to their aspirations and abilities. It is our hope that what we have to say in this book

It Takes a Village— Family Business Style

Comment from Powell's Books on the news that Emily Powell had been designated to eventually run the Portland, Oregon, company founded by her grandfather:

"While some speculate about the outcome of third generation business transitions, Ms. Powell has a tremendous support network that includes Powell's management, her parents, and the community. The announcement in Portland newspapers generated much mail from the community, congratulating Emily and wishing her well. Whether by design or not, she is surrounded by a supportive, primarily female management team that has watched her grow from a child into a smart, capable businesswoman. In addition to long-term planning, with the help of a business advisor to guide the transition process, Emily's mother, Alice, is involved in all transition and management meetings, using her training as a therapist to help address the emotional components of the process...

"Emily is especially looking [forward] to working more closely with her father during this time. 'The opportunity to learn from my dad and build on our already strong relationship is wonderful and rare.' Although Michael Powell will ultimately relinquish control of the business decisions to Emily, he will by no means disappear; he will just get back to the part of the business he loves—the books."[2]

will increase their own understanding and their families' understanding of what women have to offer.

We also hope that business-owning families, if they have not already done so, will come to a full appreciation of what an extraordinary resource women represent and what opportunities may be lost when their talent is not welcomed or developed. It is still apparent in our work that sometimes a son is being chosen over a daughter to run a business when the daughter is clearly more able and qualified. And that's when a daughter is actually working in the business. Many family businesses still have no women family members working in them at all. What talent and what opportunities are lost to those companies we can only imagine.

We encourage you to use this book as a means to examine practices and prejudices that may be influencing your family's choices, potentially inhibiting your business from achieving its own full potential. By becoming conscious of such inhibitors and choosing a different path, you can perhaps make more resources available to your business and your family. In so doing, you can enjoy the personal benefit of enhancing relationships in the family and enhancing the skills and relationships of the members of the next generation.

Notes

1. Rosen, "Passing the Torch" pp. 20-21.

2. Powell's Books, April 12, 2006. May 2, 2007, <http://www.powells.com/news_emilypowell.html>.

II.
Farewell, Primogeniture!

Family businesses are creating diversity and a broader set of leadership skills by including women leaders in the top management teams. The fact that family businesses do this to a greater extent than non-family firms could be because they have access to talented women through different networks and are not pressurized by public shareholders to be conventional in terms of board selection. It may also be a sign that the traditionally "invisible" influence of women in family firms has always been there but is now beginning to take a modern shape: as officially recognized positions of leadership.

Nigel Nicholson and Asa Bjornberg
London Business School[1]

- After 376 years in business, Avedis Zildjian, a manufacturer of musical cymbals, named Craigie Zildjian its first woman CEO in 1999. A company with roots in Turkey, Zildjian is headquartered in Norwell, Massachusetts. Debbie Zildjian, Craigie's sister, is also an executive in the family firm. In the early 1980s, they became the first women to learn the secret method of blending metals to create the "Zildjian Sound" beloved by drummers. Until then, the secret formula had been passed in an unbroken line from father to eldest son.

- Founded in 1385, Marchesi Antinori S r L, a winery based in Florence, Italy, has been run by male heirs for 25 generations. The current leader, Piero Antinori, has no sons, but his three daughters are all involved in the business and the eldest, Albiera, appears to be his likely successor.[2]

- Sisters Tami and Rachel Longaberger inherited The Longaberger Company, a popular basket-making business and tourist attraction based in Newark, Ohio, when their father died of cancer in 1999. Dave Longaberger had trained his daughters well and had complete confidence in their ability to carry on the family business. The year before his death, he named Tami CEO of the then $700-million-a-year enterprise.

As these vignettes suggest, the world is undergoing enormous changes with regard to the role of women in family firms. In some parts of the world, the rules of primogeniture still prevail, and only sons are allowed to inherit and run a family business. Elsewhere, however, such rules are beginning to crumble or have been replaced altogether.

As recently as the mid 1980s, young women in the United States often felt unwelcomed in any significant way in the businesses owned by their families. Even college-educated women felt compelled to seek careers elsewhere. Little did most family business founders and CEOs, usually male, understand that the absence of women meant that their companies were being deprived of a major source of talent.

While non-family companies began to promote able women to positions of greater responsibility and power, and while women began starting their own businesses in record numbers in the 1980s, family businesses lagged behind in making use of the tremendous resource represented by female family members or offering daughters and nieces the career opportunities offered to sons and nephews.

Family business as a field of study and consulting in the United States started when Léon A. Danco began as a family business consultant in 1962, a time when most family firms were owned and run by fathers or husbands. And that's how Danco saw his clients and audiences: men as entrepreneurs and owners, wives as their supporters. By 1980, however, when Danco published his second book, *Inside the Family Business*, he wrote of having been brought up in a male-dominated world in which the great majority of successful business owners were men:

> My knowledge and experience [were] gained in this world, but this should not be taken to mean that I ignore or minimize the role of women. It's just that I haven't had enough experience with female entrepreneurs to feel that I can speak knowledgeably about them. Women today are becoming increasingly involved in family businesses as owners and managers, an involvement I welcome greatly.[3]

He bemoaned the lack of genderless pronouns in the English language and added, "I beg your forebearance…and forgiveness. But please, Ladies, let me include you as 'one of the boys.'"[4]

To our knowledge, the first book that addressed women in family businesses was written by Danco's wife, Katy, and published in 1981. Called *From the Other Side of the Bed: A Woman Looks at Life in the Family Business*, it focused on women as the "wife of" the business owner. In a revealing introduction, Léon Danco wrote:

> I didn't even allow women to attend our [family business] seminars in the early days. As far as I was concerned, there could be only two outcomes to such a thing, and I said so. If the women were good looking, they'd be distracting. If they weren't, they'd be discouraging. Sure, I said that for effect and it got laughs, but underneath, it represented something of what I then believed.

But somewhere, somehow, I found something was missing. I found I was only hearing half a story—and not necessarily the more important or better half. Today, as far as I'm concerned, no seminar is complete, no speech is fully worthwhile, no client consultation is valid if the women involved are ignored or just kept as pets. Their influence has had a great and beneficial effect on the beliefs and understanding I have today.[5]

Katy Danco's book recounted the wisdom she had gained as the spouse of an entrepreneur as well as what she learned from the women who came to her husband's seminars. What's more, she acknowledged the shifts that were beginning to take shape:

Not too long ago, the thought that a daughter could inherit and run a family company—other than, maybe, a boutique or some other "frilly" business—was seldom entertained by business owners. If we had daughters, we expected them to marry nice boys and raise lovely grandchildren. If anybody would work in the business, it would be their husbands, our sons-in-law.

The times are changing, and we should be grateful for that. Our successor seminars, which used to be 99.9% male, are now approaching an almost complete integration. Our daughters are becoming actively interested in careers as owner-managers, and in industries which up to now were considered masculine domains.[6]

Still, no one quite anticipated the explosive growth of female entrepreneurship that was to come. Many of the women who would start businesses of their own beginning in the early 1980s were daughters who had been discouraged from joining their families' companies or who felt they could not reach their full potential if they did. They weren't the kind of women who would be content to play only a supporting role to a successful husband. Women who grow up in a family business (and listen to nightly discussions about it) may be uniquely prepared to succeed in business in a way that other women are not. These new women, at least in the United States, wanted to put their own stamp on things. They wanted to "make their own mark." Is this not what they had gone to college for?

In the summer of 1990, the then four-year-old Family Firm Institute's *Family Business Review* produced a special issue on woman and family firms. "If [research] literature about family business is in its infancy, then literature on women in family business is still gestating," wrote guest editor Matilde Salganicoff. "Serious papers can be counted on one hand. There is little demographic information, statistical data, or systematic research."[7]

In the absence of research, a chief source of knowledge about the progress of women in family enterprises has been consultants to family firms. While today consultants are seeing more women in senior management positions in family businesses including women CEOs, not long ago women were virtually invisible.

Consultants practicing in the 1970s and early 1980s noted that the subject of women simply did not come up when they met with their family business clients. The predominately male business owners didn't see the topic as important or were just oblivious to the notion that the matter deserved some attention. Fathers then still tended to sell a business or close it down if a male successor was not available.

A limited amount of statistical information on women in family firms began to emerge in the 1990s with major studies on family business conducted for MassMutual and Arthur Andersen. In a particularly interesting approach, the Center for Women's Leadership at Babson College and MassMutual Financial Group released a study called "Women in Family-Owned Businesses" in August 2003. It compared the findings on women in two other studies, the 1997 Arthur Andersen/MassMutual American Family Business Survey and the MassMutual Financial Group/Raymond Institute American Family Business Survey conducted in 2002 and released in January 2003.

Among the conclusions the Babson/MassMutual report offered are these:

—In the five years beginning with 1997, woman-owned businesses in the United States increased by 14 percent while the number of women owners of family businesses rose by 37 percent.

—Woman-owned family businesses had average annual revenues of $26.9 million in 2002 compared with average annual revenues of $30.4 million for their male-owned counterparts. The women's businesses tended to be 10 years younger than men's, however, and the women were seen as more financially conservative, perhaps curbing some opportunity for growth.

—Woman-owned family firms were found to be 1.7 times as productive as family businesses owned by men. The women generated sales with fewer median employees—26 compared with 50 at male-owned companies, the researchers explained. "[Women] do more with less," the study said.[8]

—Women took on ownership of a business an average of five years later than men owners did. The study suggested that women do not form businesses or assume responsibility in existing family firms until child-bearing and rearing years are coming to an end.

—Both male-owned and female-owned firms identified the same five industries as their primary business sector: manufacturing, services, construction, wholesale, and retail.

The Babson study also revealed a multiplier effect that benefits women: Female-owned family firms were more than twice as likely as their male-owned counterparts to employ women family members full-time and six times as likely to have a woman CEO. Women-owned firms were also more likely to have gender-balanced boards of directors.

One major lesson for family businesses, the report said, is that the way women manage seems to enable their firms to achieve greater productivity. "Learning from the management approaches of female owners may be an important future step for family business success."[9]

The MassMutual/Raymond Institute survey offered additional optimistic news. Nearly 10 percent of the responding family businesses reported having a woman CEO, up from five percent in 1997. More than 34 percent of the 2002 respondents said their next CEO might be a woman, compared to 25 percent five years earlier. In addition, 35 percent said having co-CEOs in the next generation was a possibility compared to the 12.5 percent of companies that actually had co-CEOs. Nearly 46 percent of those who thought co-CEOs were possible said that one of those co-CEOs could be a woman.

Our Own Observations

In our work, we have a chance to interact with business-owning families and to discover firsthand what changes are taking shape in their lives. Many of our observations support what the statistics are beginning to reveal. Others go beyond numbers. Here are the trends that we are seeing:

—More and more women are working full-time in their families' businesses. In the past women may have assumed that they wouldn't have a role or that their role would be very much behind the scenes. In fact, some family businesses had rules that kept women out (and some still do). But today, women's assumptions are different. They expect to be heard and to participate. Their position is, "I need to be involved. I want to be involved. I've got the skills to be involved."

—Women often have more work experience before they have their first child and stay at home than women did in the past. They are also more highly educated. A woman might have 10 or 12 years as a CPA, a banker, or a social worker before she becomes a mother. If there's a death of a key member of the family firm—today's woman is generally more prepared to step in and run the business.

—Given people's greater longevity, women still have a productive life ahead of them once their children are reared. We are beginning to see more women join or return to family businesses or take on greater responsibility once they reach middle age. Though her father had asked her to become CEO years earlier, Craigie Zildjian, resisted his request until she was 50 years old and her daughter was in junior high school.[10] But the members of the current generation of leaders are living longer and healthier lives, and they aren't moving aside to give room to the next generation. On one hand, this enables a woman in the next generation to join the business later but on the other hand, it may mean she'll have to wait a long time to assume leadership.

—Women are moving beyond such informal designations as being "the family glue" and "chief emotional officer" or "the matriarch" to being more active players. It is not that these informal roles are unimportant. Rather, we now recognize how deeply important they are and invest them with the significance that they deserve.

"Family leader," it seems to us, suggests a role with more weight than the notions of "glue" or "emotional" carry. It is becoming more and more recognized that these traditional, unheralded roles have been and are critical to the success of family firms and need to be formalized, no matter what the gender is of the individuals filling them.

—Not only are more daughters working with their fathers in family businesses but there are more daughters working with mothers. And sons working with mothers, too, for that matter. Businesses begun by women in the 1980s and early 1990s are maturing, and as the founders grow older, their children are joining in their enterprises. Soon, the first wave of women-owned businesses will become a surge of women-owned family businesses. It will be interesting to see how family business issues like management succession and ownership transfer unfold when women are at the helm.

—Family businesses are becoming more professionalized and sophisticated. In addition, more resources are available to family firms than ever before. There are books, magazines, and newsletters to be read and family business centers and organizations to join. Family members can attend seminars and courses on family business at any number of colleges and universities around the world. There is also more professional help available to family firms, not only from family business consultants but from lawyers, financial advisors, therapists and others trained in family business dynamics. All these developments can and do support the effective participation of women in family businesses.

—In the United States and elsewhere, the movement from a manufacturing economy to a service economy tends to make business more amenable to women. Nevertheless, as the Babson study indicates, women have been proving their ability in traditionally male-dominated industries as well.

A World View

From her vantage point in Switzerland, our co-author, Denise Kenyon-Rouvinez, finds that the development of women in family firms, while with similarities is somewhat different in Europe and other parts of the world. She offers the following perspective:

The Evolution of Women's Leadership Positions in Family Business throughout the Ages

The heritage of past centuries:

The wartime interim leader. From as early as the 16th century in Europe, you find more women involved and at a much higher level in family businesses than in non-family firms. Men frequently fought in wars and their wives had to step in and run the family business while their husbands were away. When the men returned, they took back their leadership role. One such interim leader was Yvonne Edmond Foinant. After her husband left for the front in World War I she ran the family equipment manufacturing company that he founded. On his return, they shared management until his death, when she resumed control. In 1945, she founded the World Association of Women Entrepreneurs (Les Femmes Chefs d'Entreprises Mondiales, or FCEM), an international organization that promotes women entrepreneurs.

War widows. When their husbands did not return from war, the women continued to run the family businesses until their sons were old enough to assume the responsibility.

Widows. Widows in many countries have successfully led family firms after a husband's death. For many years following her husband's death, Amalia Lacroze de Fortabat ran Loma Negra, Argentina's largest cement company. In the United States, Ardath Rodale took over Rodale Inc., a major magazine publishing house.

A revolution in the 20th century:

Single child. In the past when a daughter was an only child, her husband was asked to run the family business. This is no longer true thanks to the number of fathers who trusted their own blood to be their best successor. As of the 20th century, a daughter who is an only child, may find herself in a very powerful position of ownership or leadership or both. Liliane Bettencourt, the daughter of the founder of French cosmetic giant L'Oréal, has maintained a controlling stake in the company for more than 40 years. *Forbes* magazine has identified Bettencourt, now in her 80s, as the world's richest woman. Another is Antonia Ax:son Johnson, who succeeded her father as head of Axel Johnson Group, a Swedish conglomerate with interests in energy, real estate, telecommunications and food retailing that employs more than 17,000 people. Among current generation's "only children" is Charlene de Carvaho-Heineken, who inherited a controlling stake in Heineken, the Dutch brewery. She has never shown an interest in running the business, electing instead to raise her five children. However, she is reputed to be aware of what is happening in the company and is dedicated to keeping it in family hands.

Some recent evolutions:

One of many daughters. Not so long ago, there was a time where entrepreneurs would have said: "I had to sell the family business because I had three daughters and no successors." Today there are many examples like the Antinori family mentioned at the beginning of this chapter that show a different and just as successful approach. All the Antinori daughters work in the business but one of them appears to be slated for the top leadership position.

A team of siblings. In an increasing number of families, brothers and sisters work as a team. In Germany, Susanne Klatten and her brother, Stefan Quandt, sit on the board of directors of BMW. Both hold business degrees and with their mother, Johanna Quandt, own 47 percent of the company. Lubna S. Olayan is CEO of Saudi Arabia's Olayan Financing Company, which manages all of The Olayan Group's businesses and investments in Saudi Arabia and the Middle East. Her brother, Khaled S. Olayan, is The Olayan Group chairman.

No. 1 among siblings or cousins. We are beginning to see women compete openly with their brothers and cousins and be chosen for the top levels of their families' businesses. They are not only senior managers but also CEOs and chairs. A case in point is Marcy Syms, CEO of Syms Corporation, an off-price retail clothing chain based in Secaucus, New Jersey. Another is Nancy Geodecke, vice-chair and CEO of Mayer Electric Distributing Company, one of the largest U.S. distributors of electrical products.

The most recent stage in the evolution of family businesses is where families are choosing the best person for the job simply because that is what is best for the business. We are at the dawn of this stage and the examples we are seeing are relatively rare but incredibly inspiring. What is especially exciting is that they are occurring simultaneously worldwide. Just like Marcy Syms in the U.S., Mona Al Khonaini, chairwoman of Al-Khonaini General Trading & Contracting Co., W.l.l in Kuwait, or Raja Al Gurg, CEO of the East Al Group in the U.A.E.—for instance—were chosen by their fathers to lead the family business although they had brothers working in the business, even older brothers as is the case of Raja Al Gurg.

"Indeed, the face of family businesses around the world, and particularly in the United States, is changing in radical ways," writes William T. O'Hara in his book, *Centuries of Success.* "No longer is a senior son the automatic designee to lead the family firm. Sibling teams are gaining wider acceptance as a form of family business leadership, and daughters in the driver's seat are more and more prevalent. Teams of mothers and daughters, fathers and daughters, and couples running a family business are now typical arrangements." [11]

Still, O'Hara warns "entrenched traditions are not easily dug up in the Old World, which seems to have its roots in southern Europe and the Far East. Italy is one of the places where the old ways die hard, and the Antinori household is caught in a rigid system where family conventions are somewhat difficult to dispel."[12]

EXHIBIT 1 ▆▆▆▆▆▆▆▆▆▆▆▆▆▆▆▆▆▆▆▆▆▆▆▆▆▆▆

Billion-Dollar Babies
A Sampling of Women Who Run or Have Run Multi-Billion Dollar Companies

Name/ Country	Company	Annual Sales In Billions*
Marie-Christine Coisne-Roquette, France	Sonepar (Electrical equipment)	9.4[1]
Margaret Hardy-Magerko, United States	84 Lumber (Building materials)	$ 4.0[2]
Patricia Moran United States	JM Family Enterprises (Auto distribution)	$ 7.6[3]
Belinda Stronach Canada	Magna International (Auto parts)	$ 12.9[3]
Crandall Close Bowles United States	Springs Industries (sheets, towels, window blinds, infant apparel, etc.)	$ 2.1[3]
Vidia Chhabria Dubai, United Arab Emirates	Jumbo Group (electronics, breweries, distilleries, etc.)	$ 2.0[3]
Ronda Stryker United States	Stryker Corp. (Medical Products)	$ 3.0[3]
Güler Sabanci Turkey	Sabanci Holding (conglomerate in banking, textiles, cement, etc.)	$ 5.9[3]
Antonia Ax:son Johnson Sweden	Axel Johnson Group (telecommunications, real estate, energy, food)	$ 11.0[2]

Sources: [1]Company web site (http://www.sonepar.com); [2]*Forbes* "The World's Billionaires" 2007 (http://www.forbes.com/lists/2007); [3]Family Business magazine's 2004 compilation of the world's 250 largest family businesses.

Resources

Suggested Readings:

"American Family Business Survey." Study sponsored by MassMutual Financial Group and The George & Robin Raymond Family Business Institute, January 2003. Available for downloading from www.massmutual.com or www.babson.edu by entering "family business" in the search field.

Centuries of Success: Lessons from the World's Most Enduring Family Businesses, by William T. O'Hara (Adams Media, 2004).

"Women in Family-Owned Businesses," by I. Elaine Allen and Nan S. Langowitz. Study sponsored by the Center for Women's Leadership at Babson College and MassMutual Financial Group, August 2003. Available for downloading at www.babson.edu/cwl.

Notes

1. Coutts & Co., *Coutts 2005 Family Business Survey,* p. 11.

2. O'Hara, *Centuries of Success,* pp. 33-45.

3. Danco, L., *Inside the Family Business,* p. 14.

4. Ibid.

5. Danco, K., *From the Other Side of the Bed,* p. 2.

6. Ibid., p. 57.

7. Nelton, "Stepping Up," p. 44.

8. Allen and Langowitz, "Women in Family-Owned Business," p. 6.

9. Ibid., p. 12.

10. Pirone, "Craigie Zildjian—CEO Avedis Zildjian," February 18, 2004. April 11, 2005, <http://www.drummergirl.com/ interviews/zildjian/zildjian.htm>.

11. O'Hara, *Centuries of Success,* p. 43.

12. Ibid.

III.
How Women Contribute

I am a woman that came from the cotton fields of the South. I was promoted from there to the wash-tub. Then I was promoted to the cook kitchen, and from there I promoted myself into the business of manufacturing hair goods and preparations.
—Madam C. J. Walker,
Founder of a fourth-generation family business, in a 1912 speech

[Women] need to get the kind of education that would be appropriate. They need to get outside experience, away from their family business. They need to prove themselves someplace else and make their mistakes someplace else as well. They need to be clear about who they are and what they can bring to the business. It would be the same kind of advice that I would offer the men.
—Nancy F. Waichler, Family business shareholder and former board member; retired family business consultant

Women have always played roles in their families' businesses. The difference now is that women are playing more *active, visible* roles in much greater numbers than in the past and are being recognized for what they do. Just a generation or so ago in the United States, women were not welcomed in leadership positions in their family businesses unless the businesses catered to women—such as the cosmetics or fashion industries. Even then, companies such as Estée Lauder, were lead by men because there were no daughters to take over.

Now, however, we have moved into an era where primogeniture is loosening its grip and, in a departure from the past, daughters can take over no matter the industry. In the past, as we have pointed out, male founders and CEOs of family companies often preferred to sell their companies rather than pass them on to the leadership of daughters or let a son-in-law run them.

Holding a senior management position like CEO is hardly the only significant role women can play. The range of roles available in family businesses is diverse and allows room and opportunities for women with all kinds of talent and aspirations to make contributions. Some of the roles offer great financial rewards or an opportunity to exercise substantial power, while others offer enormous psychological satisfaction. Following is an inventory of the ways we have seen women participate in their family businesses. As you read it, think about the contribution(s) you, your mother, aunts, sisters, and female cousins are making to your own family business or have made in the past. Our list is random because we want to avoid implying that one role is more important than another. Each is of value in its own way.

Financier. It was Henrietta Milstein's savings from years of working as a school librarian that enabled her and her husband, Monroe Milstein, to make the $75,000 down payment in 1972 to buy a Burlington, New Jersey, coat factory priced at $675,000. Their purchase, which evolved into a retailing powerhouse known as Burlington Coat Factory Warehouse Corporation, went public in 1983, with 62 percent of the stock controlled by the Milstein family. The business remained in family hands until it was sold in 2006. By then, it had grown to 367 stores in 42 states—up from the 295 stores the company had when Henrietta died at age 72 in 2001. At the time of the sale to private investors for $2.06 billion, Burlington Coat Factory had 28,000 employees and had annual revenues of over $3 billion. The Milstein family realized nearly $1.3 billion from the sale—not a bad return on Henrietta's investment.

Countless women have helped finance startups that became family businesses by working full-time so their husbands could launch a business. In the last several decades, men increasingly have been doing the same for women.

Innovator. Miuccia Prada, granddaughter of the founder of the Italian company that has evolved into the fashion conglomerate known as Prada Group, has been called the company's "creative mastermind" by the *Wall Street Journal*. The newspaper described her as "setting trends for years" and "always innovative."[1] Her husband, Patrizio Bertelli, is the CEO of the famous firm, but Miuccia has consistently won accolades as Prada's creative force.

Step back nearly eighty years to Chelsea, Michigan, and a family business called Chelsea Milling Company. In 1930 Mabel White Holmes changed the whole direction of the flour milling business and gave it new life by inventing, in her kitchen, the first commercially marketed biscuit mix in the United States. Family legend has it that she wanted not only to create a shortcut for homemakers but to offer a product easy enough for a man to prepare. She even came up with the brand name, "Jiffy," under which such products as corn muffin mix, an all-purpose baking mix, a pie crust mix, and frosting have been sold. It's almost too complicated to mention, but the Chelsea Milling Company had been founded by Mabel's father in 1887 and sold to her father-in-law in 1908. Her husband, Howard Holmes, was then assigned to run it. Now it is overseen by her grandson, Howard "Howdy" Holmes, a former Indianapolis 500 race car driver.

A daughter-in-law provided the innovative energy that propelled a small second-generation home-furnishings business in Philadelphia's Italian Market to last in family hands nearly fifty more years. In 1934, Jeanne

Bossone married Frank Fante, who, along with two brothers ran Fante's, a store founded by their father and uncle in 1906. Jeanne joined the business immediately and, at a mere twenty-four years of age, began to lead the change it needed to keep up with demands. China, crystal and other fine goods from Europe were added, and soon, hard-to-find kitchen tools made in America joined the mix.

After World War II, Jeanne studied pastry making in Paris at Le Cordon Bleu, an experience that inspired her to stock kitchen equipment and teach pastry-making classes. Before long, she had nudged Fante's into developing a successful mail-order operation and the store became known nationally for its kitchenware and baking supplies.

"The brothers listened to my mother. She was very forceful," said her son, Ronald, on her death in 2006.[2] Fante's had been sold to a long-time employee's family when Jeanne retired in 1981.

Emergency leader. Women have filled this role since businesses began to exist. As we have seen, many women had to take charge of a company on the death of a husband or fill in during periods when husbands were sent off to war. But there also are daughters who have assumed leadership when a parent/CEO died, as well as daughters-in-law who have risen to the task after the death of a founder and the founder's son. Katharine Graham, who took on the challenge of running The Washington Post Co. following her husband's death, is certainly one of the most famous women in the category of emergency leadership. However, two other excellent examples of this role are:

—Ardath (Ardie) Rodale, who for many years ran Rodale Inc., the Emmaus, Pennsylvania book and magazine publishing company founded by her father-in-law, J. I. Rodale. Ardie's husband, Robert (Bob) Rodale, succeeded his father as CEO, and Ardie stepped in as CEO after Bob's death in a traffic accident in Russia in 1990. She stepped down as board chair in 2007 with her daughter succeeding her. All of Ardie's children, three of whom are women (a son died in 1985), are involved in Rodale and sit on its board, and in-laws, too, have made important contributions to the family enterprise.

—Wanda Ferragamo, who took over running the family's famous Italian shoe manufacturing company, Salvatore Ferragamo Italia S.p.A. when Salvatore, her husband and the business founder, passed away in 1960. She was just 38 and had no business experience. "I had not worked before. I had no preparation. I took care of a beautiful house and six children," she said.[3] The children ranged in age from 2 to the late teens.

Under Wanda's leadership, Ferragamo expanded into a diversified luxury fashion house. Wanda ran the Florence-based company until her eldest son, Ferruccio, could take over as CEO in 1984. Then for many more years, she stayed on as board chair. All of the children in this close-knit family became part of the business. The eldest, daughter Fiamma, joined at age 16 and was the only child to actually work with her father. Fiamma had a brilliant career at Ferragamo, as vice president and designer extraordinaire, until her untimely death from cancer in 1998. She won the Neiman Marcus Fashion Award for creativity in 1967, an honor accorded her father exactly 20 years earlier.

The second and third generations are now running Ferragamo. The company continues to expand and has entered such fields as perfume and even hotel management.

In the past the emergency leader was seen as a "bridge" or interim leader serving for a limited time until her husband returned from war or recovered from an illness, or until someone in the next generation could take over. As prejudices against women dropped, a woman who stepped in during an emergency could become the permanent leader rather than an interim leader. She stayed on until she decided to either move on or retire. Wanda Ferragamo served as her family business's CEO for more than 20 years. Most public companies don't keep their CEOs that long.

Back room support. How many women family members have taken on this role! They are the unsung heroines. They receive no recognition but their families' companies might not have succeeded without them. We don't know their names but these are the women who in the past served as clerks, book-keepers, and secretaries until their families' businesses grew large enough to hire non-family clerks, accountants, executive secretaries, chief financial officers, and human resource professionals. These are the women who did invisible but critical jobs, sometimes at the kitchen table—and often while they were raising young children.

The pity of this is that when a wife is finally replaced by an employee from outside the family, her contribution to starting the business may be lost to family memory. Grandchildren in particular may see their grandfather as a strong father figure who runs the business, and he gets all the credit. The young ones may have no idea whatsoever that their grandmother was an essential part of the business's success because she is not a visible business role model any longer. Families may want to consider telling the history of the family business to the younger generation at their family meetings. It also is wonderful when families write the history of the family business for future generations to read and make sure that everyone's contribution is counted, including Grandma's.

Nurturer of the next generation of leaders. Otherwise known as Mother or Mom. Wanda Ferragamo has quite obviously been an exemplary nurturer of the next generation of leaders of her family's company. One of the unique things about the Ferragamos is the lack of scandal that touches their lives. While members of many other glamorous family businesses quarrel and sue one another over issues of money and power and jealousy, the Ferragamos seem to go privately about their business. What has emerged is the picture of a family in which the second-generation siblings have understood and practiced teamwork, and where members of the third generation speak with admiration for their grandmother.

Another woman noted for nurturing the next generation of leadership was Iphigene Sulzberger of The New York Times Company. She instilled an "all for one and one for all"[4] attitude among her four children and thirteen grandchildren that continues to last and has provided the solid family foundation that has enabled the legendary newspaper and other company holdings to enjoy so much continued success. Iphigene implanted in her children—three daughters and one son—a deep love for *The New York Times* and helped them to understand the responsibility to the public that it represented. She and her husband also saw to it that the children received some financial education so that they would be prepared for ownership responsibilities. The company is now run by the fourth generation of Sulzbergers, Iphigene's grandchildren. The value of "all for one and one for all" has been passed on to them, along with a commitment to honor and preserve the *Times*. Other values were passed on as well. Members of the family were to shun self-promotion and ostentation. They were to keep the pledge of their great-grandfather, Adolph S. Ochs, that the *Times* would "give the news impartially, without fear or favor, regardless of party, sect or interests involved."[5]

Women throughout the ages and throughout the world have provided similar, effective nurturing to the future leaders of their families' enterprises. Even if they don't play a key role in the business, they play an exceedingly important role in succession by virtue of rearing the children. As they raise their children, they transmit the values to the next generation that will be so vital to business continuity and success—values such as hard work, caring about the people around you and understanding that the family should serve the business, not abuse or exploit it. To our way of thinking, raising children is a very active family business role. There should be a greater understanding of how important this contribution is to a family business. It's a role that should be planned for, thought about strategically and adequately acknowledged and rewarded.

Co-President. Many businesses are founded by husband and wife teams. Both spouses are essential to the growth and development of the business. Each plays a key role in the business. Marion and Herbert Sandler co-founded Golden West Financial and actually rotated in the CEO slot until the business was sold to Wachovia in 2006. O.D. and Ruth McKee founded McKee Foods, makers of Little Debbie brand snack cakes. O.D. focused on production and was brilliant at building complex machines to make, bake and package Swiss Rolls, Oatmeal Cream Pies and other varieties. Ruth handled the books, oversaw finance, headed purchasing and even was in charge of the fleet of trucks and drivers that delivered the product across the U.S. "If it hadn't been for our grandmother," explains Debbie McKee, a McKee foods executive vice president who runs the $1 billion company with her father, uncle, a brother and two cousins and a team of non-family executives, "we'd have been broke many times over. Granddad was a genius at machines, but Ruth kept us profitably in business." And yes, Little Debbie brand came from the name of O.D. and Ruth's eldest grandchild whose picture as a three-year-old is on every box.

Advisor and confidante. Iphigene Sulzberger stands out again as an extraordinary advisor and confidante, particularly to her son, Arthur Ochs "Punch" Sulzberger, the third-generation CEO of The New York Times Company. Punch visited his mother on weekends for private discussions about the business. He regarded her as "the one person he could always trust to tell him whether the paper was on course or losing its way," according to Susan E. Tifft and Alex S. Jones in their book, *The Trust: The Private and Powerful Family Behind The New York Times*.[6] They report that a *Times* corporate attorney, Mike Ryan, said, "Punch wouldn't really do anything of any major consequence without talking to his mother about it."[7]

Tifft and Jones have also written at length about another remarkable advisor and confidante in another newspaper family in *The Patriarch: The Rise and Fall of the Bingham Dynasty*. Barry Bingham Sr. became the second-generation owner of *The Courier-Journal* and other holdings in Louisville, Kentucky. Under Barry, *The Courier-Journal* grew in stature, due in no small part to his wife, Mary Bingham. Mary was a vice president and a director of the company's media holdings, but her major contribution was serving as her husband's sounding board and counselor. The Binghams were observed to be deeply in love throughout their lives. The trouble was, they were so close that they tended to shut out their children. Neither had the skills to nurture the next generation of the family leadership. Their children were fractious as youngsters and fractious as adults and, even though Barry Bingham Jr. had run the family enterprises for 15 years, Barry Sr., unable to achieve peace in the family, sold his companies in 1986.

A groomed CEO or senior executive. Unlike emergency CEOs, these women have been training for many years to take on greater and greater responsibility. Being groomed for executive leadership in a family business is generally a newer experience for women family members, since they have been so often shut out of opportunities for advancement in their families' enterprises in the past. Increasingly, however, women have climbed the ladder to emerge as CEO. To name a very few, they include:

—Linda Johnson Rice, President and CEO, Johnson Publishing Company, Inc., Chicago, Illinois, publisher of *Ebony* and *Jet* magazines. The company bills itself as "the No. 1 African-American publishing company in the world." It was founded by Rice's father, John H. Johnson, in 1942. Her mother, Eunice W. Johnson, is producer of the Ebony Fashion Fair, and the company also makes cosmetics and publishes books by African-American authors. Rice held a number of positions in the company, rising to president and chief operating officer in 1987. She was named CEO on her father's death in 2002.

—Sherry S. Russell, President and CEO, Alderfer, Inc., a meat processor and wholesaler based in Harleysville, Pennsylvania. The company was founded by Russell's grandfather, Lewis M. Alderfer, in 1922, and Russell recalls helping with deliveries as a child. Shortly after Russell took over leadership of the company in January 2004, Alderfer snapped up two rival companies, setting it on its path to reach a goal of becoming "a dominant, regional provider of premium meat products."[8]

—Güler Sabanci, chair of Sabanci Holding, a Turkish industrial and financial conglomerate. *Forbes* magazine identified her as Turkey's "most powerful businesswoman"[9] and listed her as one of the world's 100 most powerful women in 2006. What's most surprising is that she is a niece-successor. Despite the availability of male candidates, she was designated the successor by her uncle, former Sabanci Holding chairman Sakip Sabanci, before his death in 2004.

It is anticipated that her cousin, Suzan Sabanci Diner, will succeed her father, Erol Sabanci, as the chair of Akbank, the second largest bank in Turkey. Sabanci Holding is said to own 40 percent of Akbank.

Ascendancy is not always a straight path and not ever a sure thing, however. Abigail P. Johnson was considered a shoo-in to succeed her father, Edward C. Johnson III, at Boston-based Fidelity Investments. But after her money-management unit suffered some setbacks, she was transferred to head another division, Fidelity Employer Services. Whether or not she becomes her father's successor remains to be seen. Still, she oversees 10,000 employees, owns a substantial chunk of Fidelity, and is one of the wealthiest women in the world.

Other women are still in the pipeline and some of them are just a step away from the top position in their families' companies. It is not known whether Shari Redstone, in her early fifties, will succeed her famous father, Sumner Redstone, as head of a sprawling family media empire that includes CBS Corp., Viacom Inc., and National Amusements Inc. She is president and 20-percent owner of National Amusements, a Boston-based movie-theater company (her father owns the other 80 percent), and she is vice chair of Viacom, which owns the MTV cable group and Paramount Pictures. Her rise in the company is not without bitterness in the family, however. Sumner Redstone in 2007 settled a lawsuit with his estranged son, Brent, a former Boston prosecutor who had alleged that his father sought to freeze him out of the family business.[10] The business press was abuzz about conflict between father and daughter as well.

At age 33, Colleen Wegman was named president of Wegmans Food Markets Inc. in January 2005 by her grandfather, Robert B. Wegman, then chairman of the widely admired upscale supermarket chain. At the same time, Colleen's father, Danny Wegman, moved into the CEO position. Since then, Robert Wegman passed away, putting Colleen into the second position of leadership of the Rochester, New York, company.

Business founder. While women entrepreneurs were somewhat rare until the 1980s, such women existed long before. In 1906, Madam C. J. Walker, the daughter of former slaves, formally launched the Madam C. J. Walker Manufacturing Company, a producer of hair products and cosmetics for black women. At the time of her death in 1919, she had amassed a fortune exceeding $1 million and had won a reputation as an industrialist, a philanthropist, and a social activist. Her company was run by four generations of Walker women until its sale in 1986.

Another cosmetics pioneer, Estée Lauder and her husband, Joseph, founded the company that is now called The Estée Lauder Companies Inc. in New York City in 1946. It, too, became a family business, run for many years by Estee's son, Leonard. Now the third generation is making its mark, as three of her four grandchildren have chosen careers inside the family business. Estée's grandson (and Leonard's son), William P. Lauder, is president and CEO. Granddaughters Aerin and Jane both hold executive positions. It puts things into perspective to realize that the company Estée Lauder started—and she was the driving force—now has annual sales of $6.75 billion (2006), employs more than 22,000 people full-time worldwide, and sells its products in more than 130 countries.

Time will reveal if the businesses founded and co-founded by women will evolve into family businesses with the same frequency as male-founded businesses. Many of the women-founded businesses are still relatively young and it's just too soon to tell what their ultimate journey will be. However, our guess is that women business owners will demonstrate the same passion for passing on their businesses to their children as their male counterparts do. That was certainly Estée Lauder's wish a half-century ago and it came true.

Board Chair. You have already met some of these women—Ardath Rodale, Wanda Ferragamo, and Güler Sabanci. Some women proceed through business leadership positions to become CEO and then board chair, or sometimes to hold both positions at once. In Chapter IV, you will be introduced to Martha Jahn Martin, a high-powered family business executive who once set her sights on becoming CEO and then changed her mind. Now she thinks she might like to be the company chair instead.

In some instances, women family members who don't work in the business are assuming the chairperson's role. They have gained their competence either from experience in companies outside the family business or high-level experience in volunteer organizations. Many have also gained valuable experience on a family council.

There are rumblings of a trend toward more women succeeding to the board chair of family companies, whether or not they work in the business.

Family business board member. It should be emphasized that women don't have to be the board chair or CEO to make a significant contribution to a family business. Nancy Waichler's story, below, will show how a woman can exert major influence without running a company or its board.

We would stress however, that women, and men as well, need to be prepared for board membership. It is not enough to be an owner and a family member. Barry and Mary Bingham's media company collapsed as a family business in part because the daughters were not educated for ownership and board responsibility, and yet they sat on the board. In too many companies, we see individuals on boards simply because they are family members and owners, not because they bring specific skills, experience, and wisdom to the table.

Owner/ Shareholder. Almost nothing is more valuable to a family business than a corps of educated, reasonable shareholders who are committed to the continuity of the company. Because families are now more inclined than in the past to pass on stock in family companies to daughters as well as sons, women are increasingly becoming shareholders in their families' companies. Some, to be certain, take this role seriously and regard it as a responsibility. Others are fearful about dealing with money or are more passive, hoping that those in leadership positions in the company or on the board will render it unnecessary for shareholders to do anything but complain when things seem to go wrong. These attitudes can apply to both men and women, but there is some evidence that in the United States, many women still tend to believe that taking care of finance is someone else's job.

Suffice it to say that a woman fortunate enough to inherit shares in her family's business would be wise to monitor her investment and exert, in a constructive way, whatever power she may have in assuring its continued value. We like the notion of "involved" or "active" owners offered by our colleagues, Craig E. Aronoff and John L. Ward, in their book, *Family Business Ownership: How To Be An Effective Shareholder*:

> These owners are not employed in the business and may not even be on the business site very often. However, they are attentive to the issues facing a family business. They develop relationships with management, they make it a point to understand the company strategy, and they take the time to promote the culture of the business. In other words, they take a genuine interest in the company, offer support to management, and involve themselves as appropriate.[11]

Family leader. Like the business, the family itself offers many opportunities for leadership for women. In our experience, a family business tends to enjoy a greater chance of continued success when the members of the family take pride in the business, understand it and its strategy, and are united in supporting it. Accomplishing such family solidarity takes leadership. It may mean creating a family council, if you don't already have one, and setting up systems for communication between business and family, for educating the children about the business, for educating family shareholders, for introducing in-laws to the business, and for just having fun as a family.

Brubacher Excavating Inc., a 350-employee company in Bowmansville, Pennsylvania, turned to an in-law for family leadership when family members elected Ronda Brubacher chair of the Brubacher family council in 2005. Earlier that year, company founder Ben Brubacher had turned ownership of the enterprise over to his three children—a daughter and two sons. That, said

Ronda Brubacher, "is not a matter that we take lightly because there are lots of people depending on us for their livelihood."[12] She sees the council as a vehicle for educating the family about the business and for fostering closeness in the family. Ronda, who is in her early 30s and is married to Keith Brubacher, the second-generation president, is a stay-at-home mom rearing third-generation owners and leaders.

U.S. Oil Co. Inc, in Combined Locks, Wisconsin, takes the job so seriously that it pays a salary to its family leader, Sarah M. Schmidt, a clinical psychologist who runs her own family business consulting firm in Evanston, Illinois. As "family president," Schmidt works in partnership with the president and chairman of U.S. Oil, which has about 700 employees and annual revenues of about $1.2 billion. She calls communication her first priority, followed by family education and development.

Just as a woman doesn't have to be the CEO to make an important contribution to the business, she doesn't have to be the top family leader to make an important contribution to the family side of things. Other family council offices may need to be filled, such as secretary, treasurer, or vice president. She can serve as a committee chair, newsletter editor or run a family website. Or she can plan a family retreat.

Family foundation leader. Again, women can and do fill a variety of positions with respect to family foundations—chair, president, board member, committee chair, and so on. As we researched this book, we were struck by how many "sister acts" we came across, where one sister was the CEO or a senior executive of the company and another sister was chief of the family foundation. While Tami Longaberger is CEO of the Longaberger Company, Rachel Longaberger heads the Longaberger Family Foundation. Marilyn Carlson Nelson is Chairperson and CEO of the Carlson Companies, and her sister, Barbara Carlson Gage is president of the Curtis L. Carlson Family Foundation.

It's rewarding to give away money and support worthy causes, but it's also difficult and intellectually challenging to do it well. Maybe doing so is the perfect role for you or some woman in your family. They're not exactly representative of family business, but look at the passion with which Bill and Melinda Gates run are their foundation. Look also at how carefully and strategically they are going about the choices they are making as they seek to achieve the greatest possible beneficial impact with the fortune they have accumulated. Their approach has been so thoughtful that the second richest man in the world, Warren Buffet has entrusted the Bill and Melinda Gates Foundation with giving his fortune away as well.

For some women—as well as for some men—giving away the wealth that they have is a second career. Clifford and Kathryn (Kitty) Hach founded The Hach Company, a Loveland, Colorado company credited with standardizing water-purification tests and pioneering many world-standard water-testing instruments. Clifford passed away in 1990. Kitty ran the business as board chair and CEO from 1988, and the Hachs' son, Bruce, served as president and COO. With the sale of the company in 1999, Kitty and her son followed new careers in the Hach Scientific Foundation, established by Kitty and her husband seventeen years earlier. The foundation fosters science and science education by providing scholarships to chemistry students in universities throughout the country. Kitty is chair, Bruce is managing director.

Individual philanthropist. This is different from a family foundation in that one person—a woman of means, inherited or earned from a family business   is making the decisions about how to distribute her wealth. She needn't necessarily concern herself with the family in her decision making in that she has the freedom to choose what she funds according to her own personal interests. Nevertheless, the money comes from what once was or still is a family enterprise. Dorrance Hill Hamilton engages in major philanthropy in the Philadelphia area, and when she makes a donation and publicity is received as a result, she is always linked with the Campbell Soup Company, from which her fortune is derived.

Ambassador. A woman in this role serves as a representative of the family and its business to the community. The community can be however you and your family define it. If yours is a local or regional business, it can mean that you do work as a volunteer in the town in which your business is located. Your association with your family business is well known and the business accrues good will for the volunteer work that you do. You may also represent the family and the business at community events, such as fund raisers, a hospital groundbreaking, the annual flower show, and the like.

For other businesses or the women in them, the community can be much larger. In 1914, at the age of twenty-seven, Marjorie Merriweather Post inherited from her father the Battle Creek, Michigan, Postum Cereal Company, which over time evolved into General Foods Corporation. Because of the time and culture in which she grew up, Marjorie was—and still is, unfortunately—seen as an "heiress" rather than as the business genius she was. She was also a remarkable ambassador. During World War I, she sewed and knitted for the troops and rolled bandages for the Red Cross. But feeling a need to do something significant for the Allied war effort, she funded an Army hospital in Savenay, France. According to her biographer, Nancy Rubin, "that hospital grew to some three thousand beds and became the largest such Red Cross institution in wartime Europe."[13] It was a striking accomplishment for someone not yet thirty who was barred from serving on the board of her own company because she was a woman. During the Depression, she financed a canteen that provided thousands of meals to the impoverished and she raised money for the Salvation Army. During World War II, Post not only immersed herself again in volunteer work but also leased her 316-foot yacht, the *Sea Cloud*, to the U.S. Navy for a dollar a year. It served as a military convoy ship in the North Sea.

Estée Lauder Companies Inc. sees the world as its community, and has identified Estée's daughter-in-law, Evelyn H. Lauder, as the company's ambassador. She was persuaded long ago by her mother-in-law to join the company and she has held a number of executive positions, currently as senior corporate vice president. In addition, she has involved herself and the family business in education efforts worldwide to defeat breast cancer. She initiated a fund drive to equip the Evelyn H. Lauder Breast Center at Memorial Sloan-Kettering Cancer Center in New York City and established The Breast Cancer Research Foundation. She has worked to benefit New York City parks through contributions from two Lauder family foundations and by sitting on the boards of two park-related organizations. Harry Abrams, Inc., has published two books of her photography and Rodale Books published her first cookbook. The winner of awards in the United Kingdom and France as well as the United States, she really spreads the family name around. And by the way, she's also the mother of the family business's current CEO.

Employee. Not everyone has to be a star manager. All kinds of talent are needed everywhere. An artist. A marketing specialist or publicist. A computer expert. A buyer. A dispatcher. Every company needs competent workers. You don't have to be a senior manager to be valuable to your family business. What are your strengths and what do you enjoy doing? Does your family company need what you have to offer? If so, you and your company might make a good fit.

Mentor. Until the last decade or so, women leaders who could serve as role models and mentors within family businesses were in extremely short supply. Since women were not particularly welcome in their family businesses, especially not in management or other positions of power (board chair or director), young female family members who aspired to leadership in the family firm had to seek mentors elsewhere. And, in fact, that has only just begun to change. Women have been more likely to find mentors on the family side of a family business, in such roles as nurturer of the next generation of business leaders, confidante to a male CEO, or the "other CEO"— chief emotional officer. Since the wife could not be the business chief executive, she could be in charge of the family emotional climate, hopefully creating harmony, settling differences, and meeting the needs of family members. But this view of a woman's role did not meet the needs of the young American women of the 1970s, 1980s, and 1990s who were getting law degrees, MBAs from topnotch business schools, and advanced degrees in everything from library science to finance.

Many women in positions of family business leadership today have been mentored by fathers and uncles and grandfathers or older male cousins because there were no women in the businesses to do so. We are on the cusp of change in the United States and Europe as more women begin to take on leadership roles. Several of the women executives we have interviewed for this book speak warmly of the opportunities they are now having to mentor younger female family members in their businesses.

A Clear Pattern

As you have no doubt concluded, women in business-owning families fill many of these roles simultaneously or serially, just as men in family firms do. The difference is that women are now filling a multiplicity of roles with increasing frequency.

Once, a woman might have been limited to rearing the next generation of leaders and serving as an advisor and confidante to her husband. She might have been an owner. And she might have quietly provided backroom support in a company called "his" business.

In addition to being an innovator, Mabel White Holmes also had to step in and assume the presidency of Chelsea Milling Company for four years following the 1936 death of her husband in a grain silo accident. She, too, reared the next generation. And look at Henrietta Milstein, of Burlington Coat Factory Warehouse Corporation. She was financier, co-founder, employee, owner, officer, director, philanthropist, and nurturer of the next generation of leaders. And we forgot "employer," which is not even on our list above, and yet, as we mentioned, the company grew to 28,000 employees before it went out of family hands.

Evelyn Lauder has been a corporate executive, the nurturer of the current CEO of the Estée Lauder Companies, an advisor and confidante to the former CEO (and current chairman), an officer in the family foundation, an innovator in developing fragrances for the company, an ambassador for the family and the company, and a philanthropist. She probably fills some other roles we don't even know about.

What other roles do women play in your family business? Trainer of employees? Leader in a family office (a vehicle for managing the investments and other affairs of larger, wealthier families)? Family historian? Buffer between family members in conflict? Caretaker? (Some daughters report that they look after the needs of their CEO fathers.) Steward? Many women who step in to run a family business after their husbands die do so because they want to preserve the business for their sons and daughters. Katharine Graham makes it explicit in her autobiography that her children were the reason she decided not to sell The Washington Post Company. Knowing that a new generation was coming along, she said, "was what led me, however hesitantly, to the decision I made then: to try to hold on to the company by going to work."[14]

Bringing Something to the Table

Without question, women need to prepare for the roles they wish to play. Different roles require different kinds of skills and therefore different kinds of personalities and preparation. The size and stage of a company as well as the size and stage of a family (Second generation? Fifth generation?) will also influence the amount and kind of preparation needed. Ronda Brubacher, the young family leader at Brubacher Excavating, has only a high school education but she describes herself as dedicated to learning. She frequently reads business books, joins her husband in sessions with a family business consultant and attends educational programs at a family business center. Ronda was elected to her position by the family members, meaning she had won their trust.

Many women who end up running a sizable company say they grew with the business as it grew. When Marcy Syms joined Syms Corporation in 1978, she says, the Secaucus, New Jersey, off-price clothing retailer founded by her father "was only a couple of stores." Syms says it wasn't evident to her at all that one day she would be—as she now is—the CEO of a company with 2,000 employees and more than 30 stores. "It was just a small business," she recalls. But it seemed to her that it had enormous potential for growth, and she did want to know whatever she needed to know to be in the running for management.

Syms more or less prepared herself for each stage of growth as she—and the business—went along. Initially, she knew she needed to understand textiles and clothing, so she attended night courses at the Fashion Institute of Technology in New York City. At the University of Pennsylvania, she enrolled in the Wharton School's course in finance for non-financial managers, which she says "is still an outstanding program for managers who are not accountants but who need to know enough about the balance sheet so that they can make informed decisions."

"Whatever needed to be done at the company, I tried to educate myself about that," she continues. "I took a course in human resources. I studied with a consultant I hired to work with me on hiring techniques and compensation issues."

When it became possible for her to offer her opinion, she recalls, "I wanted it to be an informed opinion and to have a good chance of it being accepted. And I needed to educate myself in things, I felt, before doing that. I didn't feel I could just go by instinct or management-by-learning-from-my-own-mistakes, so to speak." Four of the six Syms siblings were working in the company at that time, she recalls. "I didn't feel that in my position, with other family members vying for the same thing, it would be a successful strategy to make too many mistakes."

During her first eight or so years at Syms, Marcy Syms worked six days a week and made it a point to be the first one there in the morning and the last to leave at night.

When the company went public in 1983, it began to pursue a growth strategy and Syms sought to educate herself for this stage. She took real estate courses at New York University to better understand the financing, impact, demographics, and other aspects of finding store locations.

It was learning inch by inch. "The joy was that as I learned something, I could use it and so it stuck," she recalls. "It wasn't like learning a foreign language and twenty years later, you can't remember anything beyond

'Hello. How are you?' As soon as I learned something, I could apply it, and that was wonderful."

If you are a woman (or a man) in a family business, it is wise not to focus your preparation too narrowly. It's important to develop some skills that are fundamental to any role. We would include consensus building, critical thinking, and problem solving. To that we would add the attainment of some level of financial acumen. All of these skills apply, whether you're working in the business, active in your family council, or sitting on the board of directors.

Many women consciously adapt skills they have learned in other arenas than the business world. Martha Jahn Martin, an executive at Chicago Metallic in Chicago, was a championship swimmer during and after college. During college, she won seven individual Big Ten titles and was named Big Ten Women's Swimmer of the Year in 1982. After graduating from Northwestern University with a BS in environmental engineering, she went on to win several awards for open water long distance swimming in national and world competitions.

"Swimming helped me to understand the importance of setting goals, developing plans to achieve your goals and the importance of teamwork," she says. "What I mean by teamwork is that your teammates help motivate you to go to the next level in your career. They are always there, pushing you and challenging you." A team with a very clear vision, she adds, can overcome all sorts of challenges and enable you "to go farther than you ever imagined."

Even if you are not active in the business, fundamental skills will stand you in good stead. We have heard women say they need to be astute enough to know what's going on in the business because their children will be active in it one day. They think it's important to be able to educate their sons and daughters about the business. Many women also recognize that they need to know about the business in case a husband dies or there's a divorce.

Unless they have worked in the company in positions of considerable responsibility, women who are thrust into leadership of a business as the result of the incapacity or death of a husband or other relative have to get up to speed as quickly as they can. In this kind of situation, among the best things you can bring to the table are your fearless questions and your ability to ask for help and guidance. After all, it's not about having all the answers; it's about asking the right questions. Although she sought wisdom from many people, Katharine Graham most famously turned to Warren Buffet for business advice and to Ben Bradlee, who was her first major hire and who became executive editor of the *Washington Post*, for his journalistic expertise. It pays to seek out the best.

As businesses have become more welcoming of women, and as formerly male bastions of colleges and universities, such as engineering, business, and law schools, have opened their doors to women, we have seen women become more sophisticated about their preparation. It appears to us that more women are clearly readying themselves for a variety of formal roles in family businesses—CEO or senior executive, shareholder, board member, and so forth. Some examples:

—Charlene de Carvalho-Heineken (Netherlands), inheritor of a 25 per cent stake in Heineken, the Dutch brewery, is a doctor of jurisprudence.

—Abigail Johnson (United States), a senior executive at and the largest shareholder of Fidelity Investments, earned a Harvard University Master of Business Administration. She joined Fidelity in 1988.

—Susanne Klatten (Germany), who inherited stakes in auto manufacturer BMW and Altana, a pharmaceutical and chemical company, is a trained economist with an MBA from IMD in Lausanne, Switzerland. She serves on Altana's board of supervisors.

—Ana Patricia Botín (Spain), executive chair of Banco Español de Credito (Banesto), a retail bank within Banco Santander Central Hispano SA, the banking empire built by Emilio Botín, her father. Ana Patricia Botín has built her credibility by working in the banking industry for more than twenty-five years. She is seen as the possible successor to her father.

—Marilyn Carlson Nelson (United States), chair and CEO, Carlson Companies, a Minnetonka, Minnesota-based hospitality conglomerate (Radisson Hotels, T.G.I. Friday's Restaurants, Carlson Wagonlit travel), is a Smith College graduate. She worked in the family business when it was still a trading stamp company but left to rear four children. While doing so, she engaged in volunteer endeavors that provided valuable experience. She returned to the family business in the early 1990s and was named CEO in 1998.

What Women Can Do

Women who desire to advance in the business or to rise to positions of family leadership should concentrate on building their credibility. Some ways to do that include:

—Expect to *earn* the right to the position you desire. It is not your birthright. Understand that to win people's respect and attain your goals, you have to prepare.

—Avoid running the risk of being passed over because you're not prepared. Earning degrees from rigorous schools and getting outside experience (with promotions) will help people in your family and its business pay attention to you.

—Work outside the business. Before joining the family business, gain experience by working elsewhere. Working in another business will allow you to build your skills and develop credibility. Many women work as bankers, CPAs or lawyers before entering their family firm.

—Find a set of role models. You need mentors who can help you navigate the waters of a family business. If they don't exist in your family or its business, find them elsewhere—leaders in your industry, or a professor at a business school. If you can, find women mentors to guide you through or at least include them in the mix.

—Network. If you aspire to leadership, surround yourself with people who can help you get there. Mentors are part of that circle, but so is the Rotary Club, your local Chamber of Commerce, women entrepreneurial groups and conferences.

—Think in terms of career development, no matter what role you are aiming for. Larger family businesses might have a fast-track program for high-potential people, but they focus only on developing individuals in the business. If it's not your desire to work in the business, consider how you might develop yourself for the role that you desire. Is there a career-development track for a leadership role in philanthropy? Is there a career-development track for running the family council? Or being a board member? Seek the advice of others and create your own career development program if none exists that suits you.

What Families Can Do

There is so much that a family can do to help young women prepare for significant roles in family firms. Here are the opportunities that we see:

—Start early. While they are still children, help daughters and nieces develop pride in and love for the family business. Help them understand what the business does and how it contributes to the family and the community. Let knowledge of and exposure to the business help the family attract and retain qualified members of the next generation.

—Don't leave the girls out. Ever. Even if you think the business is too "masculine." Things could change. A farming business might turn into a real estate development enterprise in 25 years' time and a daughter might fit right in.

—Prepare girls just as you do boys. Don't take for granted that girls will or won't want to be in the business. Arm everyone, girls and boys, with the same set of skills and expose them to the same learning experiences.

—Avoid creating an environment where all the role models are male. This means including women in leadership roles in the business as well as in the family. It also means including some women among your family business advisors. Girls need to see that women can succeed in a variety of leadership roles, not just in the outside world but within their enviroment. Remember the story of Powell Books in the first chapter and how, from the time she was a child, Emily Powell had women role models to look up to in her father's company? Now she is running that business.

One Woman's Story:
Making a Good Company Even Better

Nancy F. Waichler was born in 1934. Neither she nor the female relatives in her generation were encouraged to join their family's business. It wasn't that women family members weren't permitted to work in the company. "It was not something that I thought of as an option as a young person…There was never any suggestion that I might want to make this a career. Women just didn't do that in the '50s," Waichler says.

Oddly enough, however, women family members could be—and were—owners, and, despite the conventions that kept them out of the company, they found a way to make their mark. Nancy F. Waichler, especially.

The "F" in Waichler's name stands for Follett, and the family business is Follett Corporation, best known for operating the largest chain of college and university bookstores in North America and providing educational tools and services to school districts and libraries. Based in River Grove, Illinois, Follett employs 10,000 people and generates annual sales of more than $2 billion.

Follett traces its roots to a home-based bookstore, founded in Wheaton, Illinois in 1873 by the Rev. Charles M. Barnes. Barnes moved his business to Chicago and C.W. Follett joined the company in 1901 as a stock clerk. In 1924, Follett and his wife, Edythe, bought the company, and by 1930, all four of their sons had joined in, and the company began to evolve and grow. Waichler recalls that her father, Dwight Follett, and his brothers all worked very long hours. As a result, their wives began to want to know more about the business, and they began to attend board meetings.

Nancy Waichler's generation, the third, consisted of twelve lineal descendants—eight women and four men. In keeping with family custom, all were company shareholders, and so were their spouses. By the 1970s, the women in the family, influenced by the women's movement, began to thirst for more of a voice in the company and they pressed for having seats on the board.

Elected in the mid-1970s, Waichler was the first woman in her generation to serve on the board. Just a few months later, she was given a major opportunity to make a difference. Her father wanted to retire from his position as president of Follett but to continue serving as chairman. Waichler was asked to chair a nominating committee to select a new CEO.

"I think the reason I was chosen was that I did not work for the company. Most of the board members did. I think I was maybe viewed as more objective," Waichler observes.

She ran a tight ship. She stipulated that anyone who served on the committee could not be a contender for the CEO role. Because the committee did not know who aspired to the job, it asked for resumés. Five family members made submissions and all were interviewed.

"The discussions that we had were really very professional," says

Waichler. The committee members were looking for the best person to run the company. While the committee took character and personality into consideration, it avoided family politics. Waichler's brother was among those in the running and one family member later expressed surprise that he was not the one selected. But Waichler knew from the beginning that for the committee's choice to be accepted, the candidate had to be the person who could do the job and the nomination process had to be perceived as fair. Under her leadership, the committee settled on Dick Litzsinger, a son-in-law, who led Follett for the next two decades. And, Waichler says, her relationship with her brother did not suffer.

In her own view, however, Waichler's most significant contribution to the family business came in the 1990s. For background, you need to know that about two years after she was first elected to the board, the family took steps to involve more of the women. "What evolved," says Waichler, "were four seats representing the four original branches of the family, and the women rotated those seats within their branch." In her branch, the seat rotated among Waichler, her sister, and her sister-in-law. Rotations lasted two years, and Waichler served on the board a total of eight years over a twenty-year period.

Waichler recalls that their desire to know what was going on was such that most of the women kept going to board meetings whether or not they were actually voting members. And they were welcome to observe.

Women's presence on the board forced it to improve. According to Waichler, adjustments had to be made because the women were "not intimately involved in the day-to-day operation of the company. And so the board couldn't assume people knew stuff. Now that was probably a good thing because I'm not sure the board could assume that all the men knew stuff either." she says.

Back in the 1970s, the board members "were very open and welcoming" to the women, Waichler recalls, but they "had to take more time. They had to develop written materials. The board became more professional, and it needed to."

And then, to improve things further, Waichler eventually had to undo some of the very changes made in the 1970s. In 1996, she was elected vice chair of the board and charged with the responsibility of further professionalizing corporate governance. This proved to be her greatest challenge at Follett. She recalls thinking, "How do I do this?"

Follett was still run by a board of family members, and there were nineteen of them. "It was obvious to me that the board needed to be much smaller," says Waichler. It also needed to bring on knowledgeable directors from outside the family. Waichler and her committee developed a white paper on boards of directors and the best practices of boards. It was sent to every family member and, soon after, with the assistance of Craig E. Aronoff of the Family Business Consulting Group, Inc.® it was discussed at a family meeting.

Then came perhaps the hardest part. Waichler met with every woman who had served in a rotating position on the board.

"I knew that what I had to do was to persuade them to go off the board. We needed to get rid of those rotating seats," she recalls. "It was also clear to me politically that I would not be able to remove the third-generation men who were on the board. That simply was not going to happen."

The women's four rotating seats were eliminated, as were additional seats that were rotating from the Follett's family council.

"It was difficult," Waichler recalls. "It was very important for me to listen to the women. It was very important for me to understand the sense of loss that they were feeling and to reflect back to them that I understood this. It was enormously important that they understood that the sacrifice that they were making was to make the board a better board and the company a better company. And even though the loss was great—and some of them really were able to express to me how great that loss was—they understood that what they were doing was in the best interest of the company and they were willing to do that."

The board was reduced to 13, "which was realistically as low as I could get, leaving the third-generation men working in the business on the board and bringing in three outside directors," says Waichler. "I convinced the family that they could not have fewer than three—that having three outsiders was an important dimension for them to be effective." She made it clear that the outsiders could not be connected in any way to the business, and that they could not be good friends with anybody in the family. She was looking for people who were successfully running their own businesses and who could objectively offer valuable insights to Follett. For a time, Waichler was again the only woman on the board.

A policy that the third generation had put into place, when its members were in their 40s, mandated a retirement age of 65. That meant that Waichler herself had to retire from the board in 1998, and that top officers would also soon have to be replaced. Women family members began to work in the business in the fourth generation, and now there are two women family members who are both employed at Follett and sit on its board. Four outsiders now sit on the board and one is a woman. All the family members on the board are now fourth generation.

More than 100 family members are Follett shareholders, and the continued need to be sure women have a voice has not been forgotten. Other venues have been established that offer opportunities for women in the family (as well as men) to learn about the business as well as to express themselves. The chair and the CEO in the fourth generation started a telephone conference call after every quarterly board meeting, and any family member can participate in that discussion. In addition, family members get information through a company newsletter, a quarterly report, family meetings, the family council and an annual shareholders' meeting (which includes employee shareholders who are not family members).

Family members, male or female, are still welcome to attend board meetings. But with so much other communication available hardly anybody who's not on the board attends board meetings anymore.

What kind of background did Nancy Waichler bring to the board? She earned a B.A. in psychology from Chatham College in Pittsburgh, Pennsylvania. She and her husband, Richard, have eight children, including four adopted Native American girls who are sisters, so as a young woman, she had her hands full raising a family. At the same time, she did a considerable amount of volunteer work. She did not take a job outside the family until the early 1980s when she served for seven years as the executive director of a not-for-profit family support and parent education agency.

She also had personal characteristics that were valued by other board members and that enabled her to have great impact on Follett. "I think people saw me as being fair," she assesses. "I did not play politics. I was discreet in what I said and did…I've had people tell me that they've trusted me. That, obviously, was important to them."

Waichler and her husband, who worked for Follett for 38 years before he retired, have 15 grandchildren. After Waichler retired from Follett's board, she worked as a family business consultant for six years. Today, Waichler sits on the board of another family-owned company, Highlights for Children, Inc., in Columbus, Ohio.

Resources

Books and Publications:

Daughters' driving ambitions by Nancy Dunham *Family Business* (Autumn 2005).

Family Business Ownership: How To Be An Effective Shareholder, by Craig E. Aronoff and John L. Ward (Family Enterprise Publishers, 2001).

Making Sibling Teams Work: The Next Generation, by Craig E. Aronoff, Joseph H. Astrachan, Drew S. Mendoza, and John L Ward (Family Enterprise Publishers, 1997).

Mind Your Own Business and Keep It in the Family, by Marcy Syms (MasterMedia Limited, 1992). One woman's story of rising to the top in her family's company as well as her observations about family business in general.

Nurturing the Talent to Nurture the Legacy: Career Development in the Family Business, by Amy M. Schuman (Family Enterprise Publishers, 2004).

Notes

1. Galloni, "The 50 Women to Watch 2005: The Owners: 2. Miuccia Prada," p. R11.

2. Sims, "Jeanne B. Fante, 96; Built Cookware Store," p. B11.

3. "Shoes: A Love Story," October 10, 2006. March 16, 2007, <http://www.showbuzz.cbsnews.com/stories/2006/10/10/style_fashion /main2077547.shtml>.

4. Tifft and Jones, *The Trust*, p. 758.

5. Ibid., p. xix.

6. Ibid., p. 453.

7. Ibid.

8. Alderfer, Inc., "Our Company History," February 27, 2007, <http://www.alderfermeats.com/about/history.aspx>.

9. "The 100 Most Powerful Women," August 31, 2006. March 13, 2007, <http://www.forbes.com/lists/2006/11/06women_Guler–Sabanci_ E1WD.html>.

10. Karnitschnig, "Sumner Redstone Settles Suit with Son over Family's Fortune," p. A2.

11. Aronoff and Ward, *Family Business Ownership*, p. 8.

12. Nelton, "Leading the Family," p. 67.

13. Rubin, *American Empress*, p. 101.

14. Nelton, "Leading the Family," p. 69.

IV.
Finding the Right Balance:
Work and Life

> *There's guilt and then there's also exhaustion, because what do you*
> *say no to? Who do you say no to?*
> —Marcy Syms, CEO, Syms Corporation, Secausus, New Jersey[1]

A question that resonates with working women around the globe is: "How can I balance my work with my personal life?" When children enter the picture, the demands of family responsibilities compete with the demands of a woman's job and the result can be overwhelming. Some women face the additional responsibility of caring for elderly relatives. Women who work in their families' companies are likely to fare better than women who work in non-family firms when it comes to receiving the flexibility and support they need to manage very complex lives. But as women family members take on more important roles as employees and active owners of their companies, managing the dual responsibilities of business and home becomes even more complicated. The more responsibilities a woman assumes in the company, the less they can leave the job behind when they go home at night.

There is no "right" approach to work/life balance. The only "wrong" approach is not to think about the issue at all. But it's safe to say that neither all work nor all personal life is desirable for women in family businesses. Recognition that achieving balance is a constant struggle and awareness of work/life issues and possible solutions can go a long way in helping you and your family's business arrive at the approach that best suits you. The business-owning family itself needs to challenge its own assumptions about work/life balance and what it means to be committed to the business. Later in this chapter, we suggest ways that individuals and families can address these matters, keeping in mind that one of the major goals for the business is to attract and retain the best possible employees.

Three Women and Three Choices

Let's look first, however, at how three women on the rise in their families' businesses have responded, each differently, to the challenge of balancing careers they love with the needs of the families they love as well as with some of their own personal needs. Their stories set the stage for further discussion.

A "Miracle" Baby Rearranges a Career

Still in her mid-thirties in the late 1990s, Martha Jahn Martin was running the $100-million-a-year steel-processing division of her family's business, Chicago-based Chicago Metallic Corp. The youngest of six children, Martha, along with two brothers and some cousins, represented the third generation at CMC, a manufacturer of ceiling systems and specialty ceiling products with 1,200 employees and facilities and sales offices around the world. She was a vice president and sat on the board of directors and was seen as someone who could one day be CMC's CEO.

Then Martha got pregnant and everything changed. "It really, truly was a miracle," Martha says. She and her husband, Lee E. Martin Jr., a self-employed property manager, had been trying to have children for years, she recalls. Fertility drugs did not work and Martha had been told by her doctor that she had less than a half a percent chance of ever becoming pregnant. Daughter Rachel was born in 1998.

Nothing could have prepared her for the moment she first held Rachel in her arms, Martha says. "You start thinking about the fact that, hey, we're responsible for this kid and I'm going to be worried about her the rest of my life."

Before Rachel was born, Martha began talking with CMC's non-family CEO about her future. She had been running her division for seven years, moving back and forth among its three plants in California, Illinois, and Maryland. She knew she didn't want to travel so much once the baby was born. She already had someone groomed to take over the division. "Are there other opportunities in the company?" she wanted to know. As it turned out, the role of vice president of human resources for the entire corporation was available and she leapt at the chance to fill that job, a responsibility she has held since her daughter's birth.

For a variety of reasons, Martha has never regretted taking herself out of contention for the CEO position. The HR role has given her more of a voice in company decision making than before because she is involved in the all of CMC's business units, not just the steel-processing division. "Now I'm linked from a strategic standpoint into our business around the world," she says. She has also found HR to be a very powerful position because she participates in the high-level hires in all of CMC's divisions, enabling her to play a part in shaping its management team.

More significant, while she works about the same amount of time as she did as a division head—50 to 60 hours a week—Martha doesn't have to travel as much as she used to and can be home most nights. Even so, her daughter once said to her, "You know, Mom, I see Dad more than I see you everyday." So, she believes toning down her career aspirations has been the right thing to do. "You have your kids only a short time and then they're gone," she explains, adding, "I can still have a very fulfilling career, but my child is very important to me. And that's the balance I choose. It's not to make a judgment on anybody else. It's what works for me personally."

Chapter IV

The CEO door is not entirely closed. One of Martha's uncles, a mentor, said, "Still, don't put it out of your mind completely." Things could change in the future, he told her. And she agrees. But she's happy with her current role and she's delighted to see that the company's third non-family CEO, Sandra Wilson, is very talented and able and that Martha can use her own strengths to support Wilson's success. Besides, Martha says, she thinks that at some point in the future, she'd rather be board chair. Right now, she's happy that her cousin, Charles Jahn, is chairman, but if he chooses to move on to other things, she has put her family on notice that she would love to be considered for the role.

Martha's family and the company leadership have respected her decision. She did not have to take a pay cut as a result of moving from one position to another. "My dad has always been so supportive of me," she says, referring to Loren A. Jahn, who in the second generation ran CMC with his two brothers.

A Woman Forced to Cope with Special Needs

Although having a baby did not deflect Angela G. Santerini from her career path, becoming a mother did change her life and that of her family in a multitude of ways. In the year 2000, two years before being named president of her family's business, she and her husband, Bill, had their first child, William A. Santerini IV. Shortly after William was born, he suffered a series of strokes that led to developmental problems, some of which persist today. In addition, Angela's grandfather died eleven days after William was born and three months later, her mother was fighting breast cancer. The need for work/life balance and flexibility took on added meaning for Angela, who had joined the family firm bearing her father's name, Donald A. Gardner Architects, Inc., eight years earlier.

Based in Greenville, South Carolina, the business, a small conglomerate, was founded in 1978 by Don Gardner, who is now chairman. Its core business is creating and selling house plans for use by builders, developers, and individuals. A publishing arm produces a home-plan magazine and other publications, and a company called Allora, co-founded by Don Gardner and Bill Santerini, specializes in high-end custom design, construction and planning. Bill Santerini is its CEO. All in all, the Gardner companies employ about 60 people and generate revenues of $5-10 million a year. The business has won numerous industry awards, and in 2006, was selected as the exclusive home plans provider for BobVila.com, the Web site created by television's home improvement guru, Bob Vila.

But back to little William. He needed a lot of special help, and Bill and Angela moved Bill's mother from Detroit to Greenville so that she could pitch in and take the boy to therapy and, eventually, to school and other activities. William is doing well, Angela says, and he now has a little sister, Mercedes.

Angela says she has received a lot of support from her father and other family members, and from Gardner employees. Because of the demands of her personal situation, she has no hesitation about taking time off in the middle of the day when necessary. She frequently works at her computer at home at night after the children are in bed. She estimates that she puts in about 60 hours a week for the company.

Angela and her sister, Sonia G. Rudisill, who has two children and co-owns a fitness center and sports nutrition center with brother Donald A. Gardner, Jr., share a nanny at the Santerini household. Angela usually arrives home by 5:30 p.m., when the nanny, Heather Moffatt, leaves. The arrangement is not only more economical, it's more efficient. If one of the children is ill, Heather is always there.

"Bill and I are always there for dinner."says Angela. Until the children go to bed, evenings and weekends are family time—with one exception—when Bill and Angela are exercising. Leading a healthy lifestyle is important, Angela observes, because "it keeps your stamina up for the kids and your work life."

It's not just kids and work, either. There's the community, too. Angela has served as chair of her local Better Business Bureau and is on the board of the U.S. Council of Better Business Bureaus. Inspired by her son's experience and what she and her family went through as a result, Angela was instrumental in establishing the Gardner, Santerini, Gardner, Rudisill Foundation (named after all the family members, including spouses) to support children and families affected by medical disorders, illness or poverty. One of the first acts of the foundation was to donate $500,000 to the Children's Hospital of the Greenville Hospital System University Medical Center to establish the Donald A. Gardner Family Center for Developing Minds. Its purpose is to provide multidisciplinary physician care for children with developmental and neurological disorders. "That's my other real focus and passion—to help other parents or other children in need,"Angela says.

On a Trajectory Since Childhood

Emily Heisley Stoeckel remembers an event that changed her life when she was 12 years old. She was on a short trip with her father, Michael E. Heisley, Sr., and he needed to make a stop to visit with one of his employer's business clients."It was so meaningful to me,"Emily recalls,"that I said, 'When I grow up, I'm going to do something like this, something that's impressive. Work in a business like this. Have people work for me.'"

Now in her early 40s and the mother of four young children, Emily Heisley Stoeckel is a director of The Heico Companies, in Chicago, and one of its shareholders. Founded by her father in 1979, Heico is a holding company with about 40 businesses in its portfolio. The group employs between 15,000 and 20,000 people and annual revenues run about $2.5 billion.

Emily, who is her father's designated successor, began working for Heico when she was in college and joined it full time in 1991, after she received her MBA from the University of Chicago. She is the youngest of four children.

Her brother and brother-in-law work in the family business and her sister, Judith H. Bishop, is president of the Heisley Family Foundation.

At present, Emily's work consists largely of acquisitions and finance, but she has also shoulders operating responsibilities. She serves on the boards of most of Heico's operating companies, which occupy a diverse range of industries, including steel manufacturing, aerospace, plastics, telecommunications, heavy equipment, and construction. She travels weekly and typically works 60 to 70 hours a week, but that can stretch to 80 hours.

That kind of commitment to a family business requires sacrifices and compromises, especially when there are four children and a husband involved. In at least two important ways, Emily's life reflects that of her father's. First, he wasn't home a lot when she was young and he was building first a career and then a business. And, second, he exposed her to his work life, and that inspired her.

"When I was growing up, my father worked an amazing amount of time," she recalls. "I have to tell you, I don't really remember seeing too much of him, other than on weekends, until I was in high school. I always respected the fact that he was out working really hard for our family."

Like her father, she is absent from her family much of the time. She hopes her children will absorb a similar lesson. "I want to make sure that they understand that nothing in life is for free. Things come and things go, but whatever it is that you choose to do with your life, you should do it with a deep feeling of meaning and purpose, and you should do it to the best of your ability." And, she adds, that like her father, the "reality is that I work for *my* family."

But Emily also recognizes the toll this takes on her children and husband. She knew she had crossed the line when, with the help of her assistant, she was planning a weekend alone with her then eight-year-old daughter. Her little girl called the assistant and said, "Listen, I want to make sure that Mom hasn't scheduled any telephone calls during this time." Emily saw this as a wake-up message and realized she had to go easier on business and give her child full attention on their weekend together.

Emily makes it a practice to spend one-on-one time with each child. When the children are old enough, that includes taking each of them to work with her from time to time, in hopes that the magic she felt at age 12 will rub off on them. "I want them to realize that they're capable of doing anything that they set their minds to do, but they have to work very, very hard, and that life is nothing but a series of sacrifices," she says. "In a long and abstract way, that's the reason why I do what it is that I do. It's a great opportunity, but it's an enormous responsibility."

If that sounds stoic, it's really not. "I love working here," Emily says.

In addition to spending one-on-one time with each child at play and at work, Emily takes other steps as well to balance work and family life. Since the arrival of children, she has made an effort to curb travel enough so that its effect on family life is minimized. She makes a greater effort to be with family on vacations. But saying "'I will go on a vacation and not take conference calls' is a little tougher," she adds, laughing. The adjustments one makes to balance work with personal needs evolve over time, she observes. "As you're further along in your career and you're older, and your children are older and they need more emotional time, you just make it [available]," she says.

Two key factors that enable Emily to maintain a demanding career as well as enjoy her family are the support that her husband, Kevin Layne Stoeckel, provides and the fact that they have a live-in babysitter. Kevin, a sales consultant for one of the Heico companies, works from home and is much more available to the children than Emily is.

If necessary, if there were a crisis in the family that required Emily to be away from work, she says, "I could drop everything I'm doing. I have great people all around me who can pick up the slack."

Won't becoming CEO of The Heico Companies make managing work/life balance even more difficult for Emily Heisley Stoeckel? "I'm very honest when I say that my future is probably going to be more complicated and more time consuming than it is right now," she replies. While in some ways it will be more stressful, in other ways, it will be less so. For example, she thinks she will not have to travel so much. She also believes that she has to juggle more people and more expectations now than she will have to down the road.

Work/Life Balance and Family Business

For some expert opinion on work/life balance in family businesses, we turned to a colleague, Marci Koblenz, herself the mother of four and the founder of MK Consultants, Ltd., a Chicago-based organizational consulting firm. Work and life balance is one of her specialties and she has conducted a study on the topic with reference to family firms.

"Balance is subjective," Koblenz told us in an interview. She defines work/life balance as the "ratio between work time and non-work time." Balance, she explains, focuses on how many hours you are working in total and whether you are comfortable with that. "One person could be dissatisfied with their balance working 40 hours a week and another person working 70 hours a week could be completely satisfied," she says. How you perceive the role of work in your life will also color your view of work/life balance. If work is a major priority for you, long hours on the job will be less of an issue for you than for someone who sees work as less personally important.

Flexibility differs in that the number of hours you need to work to get your job done doesn't change even when you have flexibility. "If you need to work 60 hours a week and that's more than you want to be working, whether you do it at home, whether you do it in your underwear, or whether you do it on a beach doesn't make a difference. You're still working more than you want to be working," she says.

The culture of a business is an essential factor, she observes. For example, "face time" is important in companies with a "macho" attitude where one is expected to never say no and to take on more and more work. Business practices also play a role in supporting or undermining work/life balance because they affect what you need to do to get the work done. Koblenz observes that in today's work force, for instance, there are fewer and fewer asssistants to support middle and upper management. As a result, managers need to spend more time on tasks that don't contribute to business goals, such as making their own travel arrangements. This takes away from time the manager can devote to pursuing company goals—or, more probably, adds to the time needed to get the real job done.

In 2001 Koblenz conducted a survey on work/life balance in family businesses and garnered 498 responses from individuals in 26 family firms.[2] Here are the major findings of the study:

1. In family businesses and non-family businesses alike, gender doesn't matter. Men and women struggle equally to strike a balance between work and their personal lives. However, says Koblenz, women are much more likely to talk about their struggle because it's much more culturally acceptable for them to do so. This leaves the impression that achieving work/life balance is a greater problem for women employees when, in fact, it's just as difficult for men. This means that the total percentage of employees who are experiencing work/life conflict is much greater than business leaders might realize, simply because the men don't talk about it. In addition, because the women talk about their struggle and the men don't, managers are much more likely to know in advance when a woman is at risk for leaving a business over the issue than when a man is.

2. In both family and non-family businesses, work/ life balance is an equal-opportunity issue. Work/life conflicts arise not only irrespective of employees' gender but also irrespective of their age, position in the company, tenure, marital status, income, and whether or not they are members of an owning family.

3. People who work in family businesses generally tend to experience less work/ life conflict than employees of non-family companies. About two-thirds of employees in family businesses said they experience work/life conflict and 28 percent said they had such conflicts as often as several times a week. While the total percentage of employees experiencing conflict is similar to that of non-family businesses, it appears that the frequency of conflict in non-family businesses is greater. On the whole, the extent to which work/life conflict is a major problem for employees appears to be less in family-owned businesses.

4. In a family business, family employees tend to perceive the work environment as being more supportive of work/ life balance and more helpful to themselves when conflicts occur than non-family employees do. However, both groups view the family business environment as being more supportive than that of non-family companies.

5. In a family business, family employees have more flexibility than non-family members. Family members are more likely to say, "I can vary my work hours or schedule to respond to personal matters." In addition, they are much more likely than non-family employees to believe that working for a family owned company provides them more work/life flexibility than working for a non-family owned company.

6. Employees who are family members are more likely than non-family employees to say that their spouses are not satisfied with their work/ life balance. This finding reflects the employees' perception of their spouses rather than the spouses speaking for themselves. Nevertheless, it suggests that family employees experience more tension over work/life issues while there's a greater comfort level in the homes of non-family employees over such matters.

7. Non-family employees see their direct managers as more understanding of their work/ life needs while family employees regard the family as being more understanding than the managers. (The study did not ask respondents to state whether or not a manager was also a family member.)

Koblenz says the study sought to identify the "what" to see if there were differences and did not try to understand the "why" behind the findings. But, she says, "As I read between the lines in the study, I think that there may be greater acceptance of the work/life issues that employees face in a family business. Maybe that's because it's a family that's running the business and so, in many ways, [family members] are accustomed to the overlap of family and work. I'm guessing that the family doesn't come to work with the attitude that your life stops at the door, because they're coming to work with their family." She surmises that family employees are more accustomed to the integration of work and family and more accepting of the attitude and reality of today's work force that "there's a lot of overlap of personal lives and work lives and it's very fluid. Work goes home and some personal issues come to work at times."

Furthermore, she recognizes that business-owning families place a high value on the concept of family and extend that concept to the entire business organization. "Family is a priority in their lives and a priority in their employees' lives," she says.

We discuss job flexibility at length below, but Koblenz emphasizes that work/life conflicts often arise from sources other than lack of a flexible work schedule. Absence of respect for employees can be a major contributor. It can mean an employee is not treated with dignity or recognized as a whole person with interests outside the job—that is, a person who is not and does not want to be available 24/7 to the employer. To their credit, family businesses never lose sight of this fact, she says. They realize that "being an employee is only part of who this person is."

Inequities in the business environment that have nothing to do with the work itself can also be a source of work/life conflict, according to Koblenz. When, for example, employees with children are more likely to be offered flexible schedules than people who don't have children, that's disturbing to those who are not parents.

Koblenz also suggests that in a family business, it's important to recognize that family members will have a higher threshold for work than non-family employees. Family employees have a sense of ownership and are comfortable putting more hours into the job before they start feeling that it's too much and they've crossed the line from work/life balance to imbalance. And while non-family employees may not have the same interest in putting in as many hours as family members, Koblenz finds that the happier employees are with their jobs, the greater their threshold for work.

Flexibility: Handle with Care—and Wisdom

While "flexibility" sounds like the perfect solution to so many issues of work/life balance, it is not always the answer family businesses look for. In fact, it's pretty complicated. Under the right circumstances, it can be a magnificent tool for attracting and retaining family and non-family talent. And, more than ever before, technology creates greater opportunities for flexibility. Women employed in their families' businesses must themselves be responsible for making flexibility work—not just for themselves and their families but also for the business.

Nevertheless, workplace flexibility needs to be addressed thoughtfully because it can raise some thorny issues, such as:

—Do family employees exhibit a sense of family entitlement, giving themselves the privilege of flexibility and ignoring non-family employees?

—Do family members abuse the privilege? Is getting your nails done or going to play golf in the middle of the workday necessarily an abuse?

—Even if non-family employees are allowed some degree of flexibility, who gets it and under what circumstances?

Resentment arises when flexibility is handled in ways that are seen as unfair. Resentment, in turn, leads to poor morale and can hurt employee performance.

So, what's to be done? We admit a bias in favor of flexibility, because we see its many benefits: saner, happier lives for people who can modify their work to meet their life needs; happier, healthier families; stronger societies; less depression, desperation, and dissatisfaction; and better-quality outcomes on the job because employees are more satisfied and focused. As Koblenz points out, flexibility gives employees "more control over both their work and their personal life, and so it's easier for them to feel good about how they're dealing with both. In general, it makes their life less stressful."

We find that it helps to think of flexibility as a continuum in a business. It might look like this:

EXHIBIT 2

Flexibility Continuum

No Flex

Everyone works a set schedule. Time off allowed only in emergencies.

Pros:

—It's fair. Family employees abide by the same rules as non-family employees.

—Needs of the business come before the needs of employees.

—Scheduling employees is easier.

Cons:

—More stress in employees and their families.

—Rigidity may hinder employee performance.

Minimal/Medium Flex

Most employees work a set schedule but company tests such alternatives as 4-day work weeks and job sharing.

Pros:

—Fair, as long as no individuals or groups are favored.

—Reduced stress for some employees and their families.

Cons:

—Doesn't take full advantage of benefits that greater flexibility can produce.

Maximum Flex

All tools of flexibility are used where appropriate: part-time jobs, job sharing, work at home, etc.

Pros:

—Family employees take full advantage of their ownership position to craft a unique work/life balance that meets their families' needs.

—Family members serve as role models for other employees who also may crave more flexibility.

—Greater employee satisfaction; employees feel more in control of their lives.

—Further reduction of stress on employees and families.

Cons:

—Runs risk of sense of family entitlement if family members take a level of flexibility not offered to non-family employees.

—Scheduling employees is more difficult.

Source: Amy M. Schuman

What works for one company may not work for another, just as what works for one individual may not be right for another. Self-examination is necessary before solutions can emerge.

Chapter IV

What Families Can Do to Support Work/Life Balance

Business-owning families have a vested interest in being able to attract and retain the best talent available. What's more, family businesses want top performances from their employees. We would argue that family businesses that best support their employees in attaining a comfortable work/life balance are the ones who will have the competitive edge.

Here are some ways the family can begin to open the business up to all the family talent that is available:

—**Challenge your assumptions.** Understandably, families want family members to show a passionate commitment to the family business. However, such commitment is often equated with a willingness to put the business and its needs first and to work long, long hours. Family members who haven't met or couldn't meet that standard have often been viewed as jeopardizing the business. Such an assumption, we believe, unfairly penalizes women family members who, though they may be passionate about the business, have had to put the responsibilities of child bearing and child rearing ahead of the business. These family members whether women or men bring the future owners and leaders of the business into being and play an enormous role in preparing them for leadership and ownership.

The family can ask and discuss such questions as: Does our daughter or sister or niece really care less about the business than we or our sons do? Does the fact that she has demanding family responsibilities mean to us that she cannot contribute to the business if she wishes to? If she is competent, what does the business lose if we don't let her participate in a meaningful way? What can we gain if she does participate? If she can't join the business now, how can we pave the way for her entry in the future? How can she prepare for that future role, and how can we support her preparation? Is there a role she can play now?

Keep in mind that some of the most able and powerful women in family businesses today are women who did not enter their families' companies until middle age or who left to have a family and did not return until the children were grown.

Another pattern we are seeing is that women well established in their careers (in their 30s and early 40s) are having children and want a balanced work/family life. While they don't want to give up an interesting career or stable income, they are less likely to compromise on family life. Thus, new patterns of flexible jobs/careers are emerging everywhere around the globe and family businesses are at the forefront of innovation in that respect.

Shari Redstone, vice chairperson of media giant Viacom Inc., comes to mind, as does Marilyn Carlson Nelson, Chairperson and CEO of the Carlson Cos., the $34-billion travel and tourism empire based in Minnetonka, Minnesota. But keep in mind, too, that some of the up-and-comers or already-arrived have been younger women with children. Among them are

Tami Longaberger, CEO of The Longaberger Company (baskets, restaurants, a golf resort) based in Newark, Ohio, and Colleen Wegman, president and second in command of Wegmans Food Markets, Inc., a major regional supermarket chain with headquarters in Rochester, New York.

Challenge your assumptions about the males in your family as well. Many members of the younger generation, male and female, are more child-centered than previous generations and don't find the prospect of working 60 to 80 hours a week attractive, no matter how much they love the family business.

—Assess the jobs in your company to determine which lend themselves to flexibility and which don't. Obviously, you don't want to jeopardize the company, and for that reason, some positions won't be good candidates for flexibility. But more jobs may permit flexibility than you think. Examine the needs and requirements of the different positions in your company and determine which ones offer opportunities for job sharing, working at home on a computer, part-time work, or work weeks of four 10-hour days. Your assessment should be carefully done and put in writing. Depending on the size of your company, you can do it yourself if you are the CEO, have your human resources officer or department prepare it, or assign another capable employee to do it. Once you have identified the jobs that allow resilience, you're in a position to offer flexibility to employees.

—Do an audit of your company's culture to learn if it supports or hinders balance. Again, this can be done by the CEO or any capable staff member. You might get a more thorough report, however, by assigning a small committee that includes both family and non-family employees of both sexes. Ask the committee to assess informal as well as formal support, to make a judgment as to how well the company is doing, and to make recommendations for improvements justified by what benefits will be forthcoming.

—Develop a family business policy about work/ life balance. Attitudes toward work/life balance and flexibility are values based. Assigning a committee of family members to create a proposed policy on the topic will give your family an excellent opportunity to examine what it stands for and to put its values into action. Our sample policy here will give your family a starting point.

EXHIBIT 3

Hogan Work/Life Balance Policy

Among the most important values of the Hogan Family, founders and owners of Hogan Industries, is our love of and support for our own family. It is our desire to express those values through Hogan Industries by extending a commitment to our employees, family and non-family, to manage our business in a manner that supports their ability to achieve a balance between their work life and their family and personal life. We believe that such a balance will not only enhance our employees' lives but will also, by virtue of their satisfaction, be returned to Hogan Industries in the form of more productive employees. This will result in a stronger company that, in turn, can assure continued employment in our community.

In order to support the work/life balance of our employees, Hogan Industries and the Hogan Family will:

—Respect the dignity of our employees. We understand that the work they do for our company constitutes only a part of their lives. Like us, they have families and personal lives of their own, and we will honor the fact that they have lives outside our company. At the same time, we will expect that they honor their commitment to us as our employees.

—Provide as much flexibility as possible so that our employees' jobs do not unnecessarily hinder them from meeting personal obligations and needs.

—Be fair and neutral. Our policies regarding flexibility in particular and work/life balance in general will be applied and available to all without regard to membership in the family, race, gender, age, or reason for desired flexibility.

—Be diligent in seeking ways to extend flexibility and other work/life benefits to our employees. Some jobs do not lend themselves to flexibility. However, we will continuously monitor our employment positions for opportunities for flexibility and will provide information to our employees about those jobs that enable us to offer flexibility and those that don't.

—Keep ourselves as a family and as a company up to date on research and trends that offer us the tools to provide flexibility and other work/life benefits while still maintaining our company's viability.

—Not view requests for flexibility and other work/life support as a weakness on the part of the requesting employee. Instead, we will view such requests as opportunities for Hogan Industries to support our community by supporting the family needs of our employees, provided such requests are within our ability to grant without sacrificing the good of the company.

—Be as fair as possible. Being gender neutral is one element of fairness. In an effort to be more family friendly, Princeton University, under the leadership of its president, Shirley M. Tilghman, emphasizes support for working *parents*, not working *mothers*. "We think fathers should be taking time with small children, just as we believe mothers should be taking time with small children," she says.[3] Princeton's attitude is that employees can both care for their children and succeed at demanding jobs. The university automatically enrolls parents in its family-friendly programs because it found that employees sometimes did not take advantage of what was available for fear of being seen as asking for a benefit. Princeton's work/life support efforts include giving faculty members with young children extra time to win tenure.

Generally speaking, work/life policies that apply equally to both family and non-family employees will be perceived as fair. Or, if a family business retains some special privileges for family employees, it can perhaps extend different but equal opportunities to other employees. Donald A. Gardner Architects, for example, combines holiday, vacation and sick time together under an umbrella called PTO—paid time off. Employees can use PTO in small amounts at their discretion to meet personal needs, such as going to the doctor. Flexible work schedules are available to employees who need them if their jobs permit.

We also believe fairness means providing work/life support not just for parents but for all employees. "The reason that somebody wants flexibility should not be part of the consideration of whether [a request for flexibility] is approved," advises Marci Koblenz. Instead, the decision should be based on what the business needs and whether or not the person's job can accommodate flexibility. The beauty of this approach is that it removes managers from being judgmental about employees, pitting a father's desire to coach his child's soccer team against another employee's desire to train for a triathlon.

Some larger business families may also have to give thought to how fairness is extended to all branches of the family involved in the business.

—Focus on outcomes, not how the work gets done. Look at whether an employee, family member or not, is able to get the job done, advises Koblenz. Suppose your daughter takes time off early to attend a son's Little League game or she goes to the gym, but she makes up for the lost time at night or on weekends on her computer at home. The flexibility probably hasn't really interfered with her ability to do her work. If how the work gets done negatively affects other employees or if the job is not getting done, then corrective measures are in order.

—Don't micromanage. You can establish goals and timelines, but give your employees the opportunity to get their work done the way they feel they can do it best. One thing she's learned, Koblenz says, is that the more control employees have over their own time and how they do their work, the more satisfied they are with their work/life balance and the more work/life conflict is minimized.

—**Avoid appearances of family entitlement.** If family members give the impression that they deserve more work/life advantages than other employees, resentments can build and can even be detrimental to workplace well-being and performance. Ideally, family members will serve as role models for responsible use of work/life privileges. If your family business chooses to favor family employees, however, urge them to be discreet about using their advantages and to work hard enough so that non-family members see that they have earned their special rights.

—**Communicate your policies.** Recent research has found that employees frequently don't make use of work/life benefits because they don't know the benefits are available.[4] Make sure all your employees know what your policies are.

As you think about work/life issues, play to your strength as a family business. You already recognize that each of your employees is part of a family, just as you are a part of yours. You can use your respect for family as the basis for a continued search for solutions that will enable the women family members as well as other employees have a satisfactory personal life and still be a great success at work.

What Women Can Do

As the stories of the three women at the beginning of this chapter demonstrate, work/life balance can be achieved in a number of different ways. Martha Jahn Martin took herself out of the running for the CEO position and opted for a job that would reduce travel demands and enable her to spend more time with her daughter. Angela G. Santerini depended on the support of family and a more flexible schedule to help her meet the needs of a seriously ill infant and the demands of her career. Despite being the mother of four children, all of them still in elementary school, Emily Heisley Stoeckel pushes on toward her future role as CEO. A husband with a more flexible schedule and a live-in nanny fill in at home, while Emily disciplines herself to spend one-on-one time with each child.

What about you? Have you found the balance that works for you? If you are still looking for solutions for yourself, it will help to give thought to the following questions for yourself:

—How much of a priority is work in my life?

—How much flexibility does my job allow?

—If I want more flexibility or reduced hours, am I willing to take a cut in pay?

—Is the flexibility I want consonant with other messages we are sending throughout our business? (A period of belt tightening and layoffs might be a terrible time to grab more flexibility. On the other hand, it might be a great time because you might say, "Look, we need to cut costs. I'd be willing to work less and take a pay cut. I could contribute that way." It would be a win-win.)

—If my family and my manager agree on a more flexible schedule for me, how will we communicate this to others in the business?

—How would my flexible schedule affect others in the organization?

—Can I serve as a good role model for using flexibility or other work/life solutions (e.g., reduced hours or a brief sabbatical) in a responsible way?

—If I receive concessions that provide me with a work/life balance that I find more satisfactory, how will that benefit my family? The company? Myself?

These questions may be useful not only to women family members who work in the company but also women family members who hold jobs outside the company or who hold significant, time-consuming positions of leadership in the family or in the business—such as board chair or president of the family council.

If you decide to seek more flexibility, be prepared to be flexible yourself. Suppose you have significantly reduced your hours and taken a lower-level position. And suppose an emergency occurs—say, the person who holds the job you left has been seriously injured in an auto accident and your family business wants you back full-time at your old position for the next four months while he recovers. If there's a way you can swing it, it's probably the right thing to do.

Outwitting Stress

In her mid 50s, Marcy Syms, the Syms Corporation CEO and the mother of a young son, says that you feel the "same stresses when you're managing a department just as much as if you're a CEO."[5]

Although the stress may flatten out once you reach a certain level in a family business, it increases until you get to that level. Travel demands escalate, the gravity of decision making gets higher and higher if you're climbing toward the top management position, and the number of people you're responsible for, even if they're not direct reports, accelerates. If you're the CEO, you're much more visible. As a result, you become much more vulnerable to media reports about your business and your personal life. You can't even go to a party without people cornering you and asking you about your business (a fact that your spouse may find exceedingly annoying since he was just hoping to have a good time).

So, if you haven't already done so, you'll have to find some ways to cope with stress. If you've arrived at a satisfactory work/life balance, you're part way there. Here are some other ideas:

Forget feeling guilty. As Princeton's president, Shirley Tilghman, puts it: "We have to allow women to say that it is fully legitimate to be at work, it is fully legitimate to be at home—and you shouldn't feel guilty when you're in either one of those places. You do what you can do."[6]

Take care of your health. This is so obvious that we almost hate to mention it. Nevertheless, eating smart and getting adequate exercise both go a long way to making you sleep well and feel more energetic.

Investigate alternatives. Yoga and Pilates are quieter forms of exercise that promote calmness and relaxation. The deep breathing of yoga by itself can be used as a sleep enhancer. Many CEOs extol the virtues of meditation and, if you are religious, prayer can be helpful.

Check your laughter meter. Are you laughing enough? Do you see the humor in things? Do your kids and your significant other and your colleagues make you break up? If not, you may be taking things too seriously. Find ways to laugh because that keeps you sane.

Enjoy art and/ or sports. People lose themselves in one or the other or both. Each has its own healing power. Martha Jahn Martin, the former championship swimmer, still swims about three times a week to stay in shape and deal with stress.

Whatever your role in your family's business, you will be balancing and re-balancing your personal needs with what the business needs. Your life changes and your balance has to change, too. What's more, the world changes. Marcy Syms waited until she was in her mid 40s to become a parent because of the responsibilities she was charged with in her family's business. Younger women like Angela Santerini and Emily Heisley Stoeckel just plunged right in, become parents, and headed for the top of their businesses all at the same time. Whoever said you can't have it all? Well, the actress Katharine Hepburn, for one. She made the choice as a young woman not to have children because she thought she couldn't work and do a good job of raising a family. But many women in family businesses are choosing both career and children and, with the help of their business-owning families and their life partners, they are making that choice work.

Marilyn Carlson Nelson left her family business when she became pregnant with her fourth child. While she was raising her young ones, she did volunteer work, advancing to the presidency of the Minneapolis chapter of United Way and serving as chair of a task force that lured the Super Bowl to Minnesota in 1992. These experiences helped her immeasurably in becoming the success that she has become as CEO of the Carlson Companies. In her mid 60s, in a letter addressed to herself as she was at age 28, she wrote: "What I know now is that women can actually come pretty close to having it all, but you just can't have it all every day. It may need to be sequenced."[7]

A Woman's Place...

Resources

Web Sites:

http://familiesandwork.org. This web site of the non-profit Families and Work Institute is an excellent source of studies and other up-to-date information on work/life issues.

http://princeton.edu. Enter "family friendly programs" in the search box on Princeton's home page and you'll be directed to descriptions of Princeton University's work/life programs. Many may inspire ideas for your family business.

Notes

1. Nelton, "Stepping Up," p. 46.

2. "Balancing Work and Family in Family-Owned Businesses," unpublished survey study sponsored by Loyola University Chicago and conducted by MK Consultants, Ltd., 2001.

3. Hechinger, "The Tiger Roars," p. B4.

4. "Use of Workplace Work-Life Benefits by Dual-Earner Couples," May 27, 2007, <http://www.princeton.edu>. Path: Family friendly programs.

5. Nelton, Ibid.

6. Hechinger, Ibid.

7. Spragins, editor, *What I Know Now: Letters to My Younger Self*, p. 112.

V.
The Challenge to Couples

He probably would not have married me if I did not have the drive
that I have.
> —Angela G. Santerini, President,
> Donald A. Gardner Architects, Inc., Greenville, S.C.

As for [my husband], at the same time that he was building me up,
he was tearing me down...when we were with friends and I was talk-
ing, he would look at me in such a way that I felt I was going on too
long and boring people. Gradually, I ceased talking much at all when we
were out together.
> —Katharine Graham, Chair and CEO,
> The Washington Post Company, Washington, D.C.[1]

The above quotations represent two extremes in the relationships between women in family businesses and their life companions. Just as no two individuals are alike, neither are marriages or other life partnerships. Solutions that work for one couple may not work at all for another. The values that one couple holds dear may have little priority in the relationship of another. Nevertheless, there are things we have observed in and learned from the unions of women in family businesses and their significant others.

Before we move on, we want to make it clear that our observations are not limited to traditional marriages involving a husband and a wife. We are also talking about domestic partnerships and same-sex couples. We are seeing more and more of these relationships in business-owning families in our consulting work as more and more families acknowledge their existence and extend a welcome. If we sometimes use the words "spouse," "husband," "wife," or "marriage," please accept it as a form of shorthand.

We have found that there are three major issues that must be dealt with to the reasonable satisfaction of both partners in many, if not most, relationships involving a woman who is part of a business-owning family. These are wealth, work/life balance, and how—in view of a woman's success or advantages—a couple deals with self-esteem issues. All of these issues bleed into and affect one another. We address work/life balance at length in Chapter IV. In this chapter, we focus on it specifically as it affects a couple's relationship.

Facing Up to Wealth

When a woman brings more assets into a marriage than her partner does, difficulties can ensue, particularly if the woman is of considerable wealth. The wives' wealth undermined the marriages of two highly visible women from family businesses: Katharine Graham, former CEO of the Washington Post Company, and Iphigene Ochs Sulzberger, the second-generation matriarch of the clan that runs the New York Times Company.

Because of the times in which these women grew up, neither of their fathers considered bringing their daughters into their companies and grooming them for leadership. In both cases, the fathers hired their daughters' husbands, and both these sons-in-law eventually took over leadership of their wives' family businesses. Graham's father transferred more stock to her husband, Philip Graham, than he did to his own daughter because, she said, "as Dad explained to me, no man should be in the position of working for his wife. Curiously I not only concurred but was in complete accord with this idea."[2]

Talented though both the husbands were, each seemed to have a nagging suspicion that he had gotten where he was because he had married the boss's daughter. In her autobiography, *Personal History*, Graham recounts how her husband belittled and humiliated her, chipped away at her self-confidence, and engaged in a long-running affair. His mental health deteriorated and he died by his own hand in 1963, leaving his wife a widow at 46 with four children and a media company to run.

Somewhat like Phil Graham, Arthur Hays Sulzberger demeaned his wife, Iphigene, and sought refuge with women outside their marriage. Iphigene's story is thoroughly explored in *The Trust: The Private and Powerful Family Behind The New York Times*, by Susan E. Tifft and Alex S. Jones. Like Katharine Graham, Iphigene Sulzberger hid her light under a bushel in an attempt to bolster her husband's ego and preserve her marriage. It's a dynamic that's not uncommon when sons-in-law are brought into family businesses and promoted to significant levels of responsibility. "Did I achieve my success on my own or did I only achieve it because I married the owner's daughter?" these men ask themselves, and the very question claws at their self-esteem.

Another instructive tale is that of Marjorie Merriweather Post. In 1914, at age twenty-seven, Post became one of the world's richest women when she inherited her father's business, the Postum Cereal Company in Battle Creek, Michigan. In those days, it just wouldn't do for a woman to run the company but Post was a very smart heiress, at first making major decisions from afar through an uncle, who served as Postum's chairman, and her first husband, who represented her on the board of directors. Her second husband was noted stockbroker E.F. Hutton, who became chairman of the board and took Postum public. Postum eventually evolved into what is now General Foods Corporation.

Chapter V

In all, Post had four husbands and each marriage ended in divorce. Her wealth itself was not considered the overriding factor in any of her divorces. She grew apart from her first husband. She couldn't bear the infidelity of her second husband, Hutton, who was a great success in his own right and who had advanced her fortune considerably. Her third husband, once the ambassador to the Soviet Union, grew cantankerous and possessive, and jealous of the fact that while his own prominence was declining, hers was on the rise. Her last husband, a successful and well-liked business executive, turned out to have an incompatible sexual orientation.

Her biographer, Nancy Rubin, writes that some blamed Post's adulation for her father for the failure of her marriages while others felt she just had bad luck in her choice of husbands. "Others," writes Rubin, "believed that Marjorie's physical and financial assets were just too much for any man to handle." She was described as having "twice the life force" of two of her mates.[3]

As Marjorie Merriweather Post's life suggests, it's probably unwise to look at a woman's wealth as the sole cause of a marital breakdown. Nevertheless, the accoutrements of wealth and the values they represent can provide clues to what can go wrong in a relationship. As she grew older, Rubin says, Post became "less likely to allow her husbands to carve out 'space' for themselves."[4]

These stories remind us how far women from business-owning families in many parts of the world have come in the last several decades. Today, the fathers of Katharine Graham, Iphigene Sulzberger, and Marjorie Merriweather Post may well have welcomed their daughters, all brilliant, into the family business and hailed the possibility that they would one day run the show. In fact, Sulzberger and Post were only children and their fathers took great pains to prepare them for ownership. Yet, as grownups, these daughters had to exert their business leadership indirectly, primarily through male family members. While Graham was not as well prepared for business ownership, she was the only one of the three women to become the leader of her family's company. Once in the driver's seat, she became one of the most respected CEOs in the United States. As her son, Donald E. Graham, has pointed out, The Washington Post Company went public under her leadership in 1971. She "would go on to increase the stock price by more than 4,000% in the next 20 years," he said.[5]

Not all women in business-owning families bring more assets into a relationship than their partners do. When she and her husband, Bill, joined Donald A. Gardner Architects in the early 1990s, Angela Santerini recalls, the company had five employees. What wealth the Santerinis have accumulated they have built together with Angela's father.

Martha Jahn Martin and Emily Heisley Stoeckel, coming from much larger companies, both acknowledge that they brought greater financial resources into their marriages than their husbands. The wealth itself doesn't cause problems, Heisley Stoeckel says, but it does cause her husband to ask why, given its existence, she works so hard. "To be perfectly honest, our biggest issue is that I work a lot," she says.

Martin says the matter of her wealth has not caused problems in her marriage "because my husband and I are very open. I've always shared everything with him." Lee Martin takes care of the bills and they have only one checking account. Except for two trusts that are kept separate for tax purposes, they share everything jointly.

The Martins never discussed the matter of Martha's wealth before they married and they don't really talk about being wealthy now, she says. "We don't live a very wealthy lifestyle. We're constantly investing our money back and thinking about the future." They do have a summer home in Cheboygan, Michigan, however, and, for Lee's 46th birthday, they got something he'd been wanting at least since his 40th: a Ford Mustang.

They share tasks—he does the cooking, she does the cleaning, and they do the laundry together with their daughter, Rachel. With her resources, Martha does the cleaning??? "Yes, I do," she replies. "I could find someone [to do it] but I just haven't gotten around to it." Because Lee is self-employed and has more flexibility, he drives Rachel most of the places she needs to go during the week and Martha does most of the chauffeuring on weekends.

Santerini, Heisley Stoeckel, and Martin offer a bright picture of couples coping with a woman's wealth and a high-flying career. For other couples, dealing with a woman's wealth is a struggle, whether or not she works in the business. It's a struggle not just for the couples themselves but also for many business-owning families. In many places around the world today, wealth no longer goes just to the sons or just to the firstborn son. Parents love all their children equally and want to be egalitarian in passing assets to them. Even as they channel significant wealth to their sons and daughters, parents worry about protecting the family's assets. They may pressure their children to sign prenuptial agreements that will preserve the wealth for the family and prevent it from falling into the hands of daughters- and sons-in-law in the event of divorce. When it comes to sizing up their children's potential marital partners, parents in family businesses may also become overprotective of their offspring, especially of daughters. We have often seen that even family business advisors worry about who the women in a family business will marry—often more than they worry about the women themselves.

One reason people experience discomfort when a woman brings more assets into a relationship is that doing so is still untraditional. Despite the fact that in dual-income marriages one out of four women in the United States now out-earn their husbands,[6] we are still not used to the idea.

It may be surprising, but we often find that even though they may have significant wealth and even though they are more empowered than ever, many women still assume that someone will "take care of them" because that's what they were brought up to expect. In such cases, women may believe it's the husband's responsibility to manage the money and, because this attitude is so prevalent, women can be less attentive to finances than they should be—or not attentive at all. Families collude by not teaching their daughters about managing money and thereby leave their daughters vulnerable to the very scheming, gold-digging husbands from which the family had hoped to protect their daughters. We will cover becoming financially literate in the next chapter.

Wealth also amplifies and magnifies other issues in a relationship. Ordinarily, for example, the matter of gift giving seems harmless. When a woman's wealth or her family's resources far exceed the level of cash in her husband's family, however, gift giving becomes a minefield. The couple has to avoid being overly generous to the members of the husband's family because they can't reciprocate in kind and may feel resentful. Or the husband's parents may think their son and particularly his rich wife are showing off with their generous gifts. But the husband's family will also feel resentful if the couple seems stingy. It's a fine line to walk.

Money also raises issues of control. Who makes the decisions? Does the woman make the decisions or try to control her partner because she is wealthier or makes more money? Or does her partner try to wrest control as a means of shoring up his ego?

Wealth, or rather the husband's lack of it, can raise some issues of respect. Consider this scenario: Serena, the daughter of Harvey, a hard-driving, well-heeled business owner, marries a pleasant, unassuming teacher we'll call Ted. The young husband never expects to be anything other than a high school science teacher because he enjoys his career. What's more, Ted's father is a barber and his mother is a school secretary. Unlike his wife, who has already received substantial gifts of stock from her father and who will likely inherit much more, Ted brings only his modest savings and his golden retriever into the marriage. Harvey can't reconcile himself to the match. He frequently needles Serena about her "dependent" husband and asks her when Ted is going to get a real job. Or he demeans Ted directly, under the guise of teasing. Harvey is challenging Ted's manhood, but if Ted bristles or protests, Harvey says, "What's the matter? Can't you take a joke?"

In some cases, the inability of a couple to deal with the issue of the woman's wealth can even lead to the dissolution of a relationship.

Responsibilities vs. Life Partners

Women with soaring careers in family businesses or significant family business governance responsibilities (board chair or president of the family council) have limited time to devote to life partners let alone children. Like Emily Heisley Stoeckel's husband, their partners may wonder why their wives work so hard when, from a financial standpoint, they don't need to.

But like Heisley Stoeckel, the women are passionate about what they do. "I have to tell you that I believe it's part of my identity," says Heisley Stoeckel. "I take great pride in the fact that I am part of an amazing team of people who have created this value."

She also points out that her job requires "countless" hours. Of her husband, she says, "I'm not saying that he always likes it, but he does accept it."

"I think that I have a lot of freedom because I work for myself," she adds, "but I think that I have a tremendous number of demands that prevent me from taking advantage of that."

While she believes her husband is proud of her, she says, "Sometimes it's difficult because when you step into business mode, your mind and your focus is completely separate from your family." Work can intrude on the couple's social life. They might go to a party, for example, and someone will come up to them and start to talk with Emily about business. "All of a sudden, I become engaged in it."

Success and Self-Esteem

Women in business-owning families can be wealthy and powerful. They may be rising stars in the corporate world. Perhaps they are idols of young women and girls seeking to emulate them. Surely they are role models.

All this can be unnerving to their significant others. Men, particularly more traditional ones, may experience a loss of self-esteem or self-confidence when they feel that they're just seen as an attachment to a wealthy or powerful woman. That can put pressures on a marriage and a couple has to be prepared to deal with those feelings. A woman may feel that she needs to take a second position, lest she emasculate her husband or convey the impression that he's not capable. In the process, she loses her own self-assurance and the family and its business experience the loss of much or all that she could contribute.

Fortunately, many younger men these days are more used to successful women. They've met high-achieving women in college, graduate school or after graduation. They've worked with them on the job. So it's no surprise to them that their wives are successful.

Martha Jahn Martin reports that her husband, handles her success by always being encouraging. "[He] tells me to 'go for it! Go get 'em!' He's a very positive person."

Asked if friends tease her husband and imply that she wears the pants, Martha answers that people don't say such things to his face but he knows that people talk about the fact that, because Martha makes a good living, they enjoy certain advantages. People can be a little jealous at times, she says. "And he is sensitive to that. That does bother him. But I tell him, 'You can choose to be sensitive to that or not. What's important is how you feel inside.'...We talk about it. And that's something *he's* got to work through."

EXHIBIT 4

What Kind of Man Does It Take?

We asked Angela Santerini, Martha Jahn Martin, and Emily Heisley Stoeckel what kind of man it takes to be married to women who are wealthy and/or powerful in family businesses. Here are their thoughts. What do you think?

—Has a strong sense of self-esteem.

—Is patient.

—Can tolerate interruptions.

—Has interests separate from your own (which might also be complementary to yours).

—Is successful in his own way—not necessarily monetarily. It could mean successful in giving back to society.

—Is a positive person.

—Enjoys offering encouragement and support.

What Couples Can Do

First, celebrate what each of you brings to the relationship, whether it's intelligence, a great sense of humor, an adventurous nature, a love of kids and animals, a warm smile, leadership skills, wealth, good looks or a good heart.

Next, know that nothing beats good communication between life partners. That means being open, trusting, and respectful, and being able to talk about difficult subjects.

When a woman brings more assets into the relationship or makes more money or has more power in her job, it helps if both partners understand that they are in a situation different from the societal norm and can talk about what that means. What are the risks of being untraditional? The rewards? How does it make each of us feel?

As a couple, you should explore your attitudes toward money and how you're going to make financial decisions. You can have conversations around such questions as: What are our financial goals as a couple? How are we going to increase each other's net worth? How are we going to protect both of our financial interests and not just the one who brings the most assets into the relationship? How can we both take responsibility for our finances? How do we make major purchasing decisions? Is money being used as a means of control? How can we make things fairer? The resources listed at the end of the chapter can provide additional ideas for having conversations about money and wealth.

Work on making decisions as a team, not just financial decisions but life decisions such as where to live, where to send the children to school, how to support each other's aspirations, and what to do on Saturday night. (If she thinks she should work and he thinks they need a night out together, this can become an important decision.) We've heard of husbands who decide on their own to move the whole family to another community or even to another part of the country and expect their wives to go along with that decision. That hardly constitutes teamwork and surely can harm their relationships.

Making decisions as a team reduces the possibility that one partner or the other will attempt to seize control. You don't want the wife saying, "Well, it's my money so I get to decide where we go on vacation or what type of home we have." And if her partner can demonstrate a sense of appreciation and respect for the fact that the money originates with her, the more she will be willing to allow for team decision making as opposed to wanting to be in control.

What Women Can Do

As they work out their work/life balance issues, women need to consider not just their family as a whole but their husbands or life partners in particular. As Emily Heisley Stoeckel mentioned, the amount of time she spends working tends to be a sore point with her husband. Obviously, it's important to nurture the relationship with one's significant other. Angela Santerini and her husband plan two vacations a year—one with the children and one for just themselves.

Showing appreciation for what a partner brings to the table is invaluable to a relationship. Martha Jahn Martin, whose husband fills in with a lot of the home tasks, says, "I know he does so many things to support me and to support our family and to take care of the house so that I don't have to worry about those things." If he wants to go off on a short vacation to visit a friend or pursue one of his passions, snowmobiling, she encourages him to do it. That's one way she shows him her appreciation, and she knows there will be times when she has to travel on business and he'll have to take care of their daughter.

What Husbands and Life Partners Can Do

Not all women who are part of business owning families are well off. Many times a family's greatest asset is their business and that wealth may be illiquid.

If your partner has substantial assets, focus on the positive aspects. Does her wealth provide you with greater freedom and opportunities? Can you work less, if that's your desire, and volunteer more? What other benefits does wealth offer? If she's not working in the business, can you work together on projects that can make a difference in your community or enjoy travel together?

Do something that gives your life meaning. If your partner's financial means enables you to do that, so much the better—it will add to her sense of purpose, too. Consider Bill and Melinda Gates and how the wealth that Bill has built through Microsoft now enables them both through their foundation, to make a real impact on world health and other major issues.

If your spouse is working in the business and experiencing extraordinary demands on her time, show her that you appreciate the sacrifices she is making for you and the family. If you are both engaged in demanding jobs, work together to find solutions that will reduce your stress and enable you to spend more time with each other and your children. Should you hire a housekeeper? A nanny? Someone to do the yard work?

If you are feeling any self-doubts stemming from your partner's position or her wealth and these feelings persist, it's perhaps time to visit with a therapist or a consultant trained to help individuals deal with such issues. While wealth in itself is a neutral commodity wealth can be a point of friction for many people, and some skilled and sensitive professionals have emerged to provide wisdom and guidance surrounding wealth issues. Again, you'll find sources at the end of this chapter.

What Families Can Do

Instead of trying to protect daughters from men attracted to them for their money, business-owning parents can take steps to arm their daughters with the knowledge they need to protect themselves. Encourage the young women in your family to learn to be responsible for their own finances, whether or not they work in the business. Let them know, by word and example, that if and when they marry, they should regard finances as a joint responsibility. Families can do much to mentor female members and to help them build self-confidence in the arena of money management. Families can also help young women and their chosen partners deal with issues of wealth. The following story offers an example:

> Sylvie, approaching thirty-five, had spent the last five years as a free-lance journalist with aspirations to blend a career with her desire to start a family. Her family's business, now in its fourth generation, had made it possible for her to pursue work and travel as she pleased. She received a director's fee, shareholder dividends, and monetary gifts from her parents. She knew her family had means that others did not.
>
> Sylvie was becoming increasingly involved with Nathan. But, not surprisingly, as they became more serious about each other, things began to grow awkward and

uncomfortable between them. Nathan was a successful project superintendent for a local ironworker. His company specialized in custom ornamental metal for high-end consumers. The creations were works of art that required extensive time and attention to detail. For weeks at a time, Nathan's days and evenings could be consumed with designing and then preparing and forging iron to meet client deadlines, and developing younger, less-experienced craftsmen who apprenticed under him.

Nathan's responsibilities prevented him from taking extended time off. He lived simply and when time became available, he enjoyed remaining local.

Sylvie's family and its business, on the other hand, had her traveling several times a month for board meetings, shareholder meetings, family council meetings, and the various committees associated with each one. She had access to the family's vacation spots in the Colorado and the Caribbean, with an airplane available as necessary. She wanted to learn and to stay current with developments at the business so that she could be a better director and owner. Sometimes that meant traveling to conferences and courses related to finance, strategy, and governance issues. In addition, she was often away on free-lance assignments.

Putting this all in perspective for Nathan was proving difficult. Sylvie often downplayed her family's wealth, leaving out details that suggested conspicuous consumption or emphasized leisure. She had always expected to disclose her situation to a potential spouse, but doing so became more awkward the longer she waited. When exactly do you say, "Oh, by the way, there's this fund… ," without introducing some mistrust and confusion?

Sylvie's family was supportive and willing to help. The family council created an orientation program designed for future in-laws that acquainted them with the business. The council developed a family participation agreement describing the circumstances under which in-laws could work in the business, attend family council meetings and education sessions, serve on the board, and participate in the family foundation. The program included time with financial advisors who could discuss with both Sylvie and Nathan their future financial situation. The advisors reviewed the mechanics of the trusts for Sylvie as well as trusts for the couple's future children, and assisted the couple in creating net worth-building opportunities for Nathan.

Finally, Sylvie and Nathan acknowledged the unconventional nature of their disproportionate means. They agreed to meet with a specialist who could facilitate their discussions about work/life balance, merging different lifestyles, their assumptions about shared assets, Sylvie's "dominant" role as the main source of income in the relationship, and Nathan's need to keep active in his trade.

With the support from the family and accurate information on the table, Nathan and Sylvie were now able to have useful conversations about financial goals; values surrounding work, life, and money; their individual professional pursuits; and merging their lives. Sylvie agreed to focus on her family business responsibilities as a means of reducing her time away from home. Nathan decided to establish his own design studio to concentrate on the custom jobs he really loved. By depending on adequate managers and apprentices, he saw that he could reduce his work load and join Sylvie on more travel.

As this story shows, a family can be essential in helping couples find satisfactory solutions for troublesome issues.

And what if your daughter is being groomed to run your company one day and the love of her life is her polar opposite? Your daughter runs a mile a minute. She's assertive and smart. In short, she's an up and comer. He's a great guy but not as ambitious. You might wonder about her choice, but if your daughter is as smart as you think she is, she is probably smart enough to choose her own life partner. Respect her decision, and treat her partner with respect. He may be just what she needs to give her balance, to offer a break from the stresses and demands of business, and to provide the support on the home front that is needed so that she can do the job you want her to do in your business.

Resources

Books:

Personal History, by Katharine Graham (Knopf, 1997). Includes an in-depth look at a marriage that went wrong and how Graham overcame it to become one of America's most highly respected CEOs.

Smart Couples Finish Rich, by David Bach (Broadway Books, 2001). Shows couples how to take a teamwork approach to finances while nourishing the relationship at the same time.

Why Me? Wealth: Creating, Receiving and Passing It On by Denise Kenyon-Rouvinez, Thierry Lombard, Matthiew Ricard, John L. Ward and

Gabs (Family Enterprise Publishers, 2007). With insight, wisdom and humor this book provides important questions as well as clear guidance on the subject of the generational transition of wealth.

Information and Referrals:

American Association for Marriage and Family Therapy, 112 South Alfred Street, Alexandria, Virginia 22314-3061; (703) 838-9808 or www.aamft.org. Offers books and publications plus an online referral service, www.therapist locator.net/, which enables you to search for a therapist near you.

Prenups or No?

If you're not yet married but thinking about it, the issue of a prenuptial agreement may come into play. Some business-owning families insist on prenuptial agreements as a way to protect the family's assets. However, prenups can be intimacy-robbing mechanisms that send messages with unpleasant connotations: "I love you but I don't trust you." Or, "My family and I need to be in control here." Prenups have to be handled gingerly and sensitively. If they are used, it should be a family's policy that all the members of the next generation will have one and that a prenup will not be unique just to one couple. Then a woman can say to her intended, "To protect our family's assets, my family has a policy that requires me and all of my siblings and cousins to have prenuptial agreements." Putting it that way helps her fiancé to understand that he is not being singled out as someone who is not to be trusted.

Notes

1. Graham, K., *Personal History*, p. 231.

2. Ibid., p. 181.

3. Rubin, *American Empress*, p. 353.

4. Ibid.

5. Ibid.

6. Graham, D., "The Gray Lady's Virtue," p. A17.

7. United States Department of Labor. Bureau of Labor Statistics. "Women in the Labor Force: A Databook," 2006. May 27, 2007, <http://www.bls.gov/cps>. Path: Economic News Releases, Reports and Summaries, "Women in the Labor Force: A Databook," Table 25, "Wives who earn more than their husbands, 1987-2004."

VI.
Becoming Financially Literate

I lost my father unexpectedly. He collapsed in an airport and never regained consciousness. I was the only one who could take over the family business and I was immediately confronted with decisions that were overwhelming. I was grieving, lonely, and frightened.
— A family business daughter

She had run companies and managed their budgets, but Liz Perle finally had to admit that she had an unhealthy attitude toward her own finances. She had never balanced a checkbook. "I realized that I didn't open my statements from the mutual funds people, that I didn't open my Visa bills."[1]

She recognized that many women have conflicted feelings about money and are fearful of dealing with it. So she decided to explore women's reluctance to manage their personal finances in a book, *Money, a Memoir: Women, Emotions and Cash*. She talked to numerous women about the topic and, in an interview, she told *Publishers Weekly* magazine that one of the most disturbing discoveries was "how quickly women sell themselves out. How little women really value their time and their contributions. And it broke my heart."[2]

It's not at all unusual for women, even the brightest and wealthiest, to resist learning about their personal finances let alone managing them. However, overcoming your misgivings and taking charge of the financial aspects of your life are some of the most responsible steps you can take. You will find that doing so gives you greater self-confidence than you ever had before, along with increased power, knowledge and independence to make decisions about your own life and most likely the lives of your children.

Citing studies by the U.S. Bureau of Labor Statistics and the National Center for Women and Retirement, Perle offers these figures:

—Nine out of 10 women can expect to be financially independent during some point in their lives.[3]

—Women make up 87 percent of the impoverished elderly.[4]

—More than 54 percent of the women in one study put off making a financial decision because they were afraid of making a mistake; 58 percent said they didn't know how to make and manage investments.[5]

These statistics point to the need for women to have an understanding of money and how to deal with it.

Some readers may find it strange that in this day of the liberated, talented, powerful female, there are women still in the dark about finances. In our experience, however, there are many such women. Some, 45 years and older, were conditioned from early childhood to believe that managing finances was the man's job, whether that man be father, husband, or a family advisor, such as a lawyer, banker, or accountant. These women saw their duty as taking care of the household and the children while their husbands took care of the business and the check book. When their husbands pass away, they're lost. They have no idea how to manage daily operating expenses, but they may be forced to make decisions about the business that they are not capable of making. As a result, they may rely on the guidance of advisors who are not fully committed to their best interests. Divorce can also leave a woman financially stranded unless she has made herself knowledgeable and has taken precautions to protect her own interests.

In some cultures within the United States and around the world, women of all ages are expected to let the men handle the family finances. Should a husband or father die, a wife or daughter may end up dependent on a brother or other male relative.

But even when young women are trained and are expected to have careers, we find that they sometimes have not educated themselves about finances. They may have had credit cards, but their bills were paid by their parents. When they get their first home or apartment, they realize that the financial aspect of their lives is much more complicated than they had expected.

Whether you are a shareholder or employee of a family business, the spouse of a family business owner, or a stay-at-home mom in a business-owning family, it is critical that you gain a substantial understanding of your personal and business finances. You also should understand how the finances of the family and of the business intersect. This does not mean you have to go back to school and take courses in accounting and finance or get a business degree. Below, we describe specifically what we think you ought to know (and why you ought to know it), and we offer ideas for how you can go about getting the knowledge that you need. At the end of the chapter, you will find a list of useful resources for getting and maintaining your financial education.

What You Need To Know About Family Finances

On the family side of things, every woman needs to be familiar with two things: (1) the Family Balance Sheet, and (2) the Family Income Statement. While our discussion here focuses on a couple's need to share and understand this information, it goes without saying that even single, self-supporting women needs to understand this facet of their own finances.

1. The Family Balance Sheet. Simply put, this means, "What do we own and what do we owe?" A Family Balance Sheet is a snapshot of your financial condition at a moment in time. A balance sheet offers an excellent place to start understanding your personal financial situation. You can use it to initiate conversations with your spouse that can increase your understanding of what you own, what kind of debts you have, and where you would find cash if you needed it quickly. Discussions about your balance sheet will help you see your family's financial strengths and weaknesses and help you set and monitor goals.

Here is a sample of a Family Balance Sheet. Use it as a guide to develop one that reflects your particular situation.

EXHIBIT 5

Family Balance Sheet

Family Assets
(What you own and its current value)

Cash in the bank	$ 50,000
Cash in other places	25,000
Loan to the family business	100,000
Stocks and bonds	300,000
Company pension funds	250,000
401k retirement plans	400,000
Primary residence	500,000
Florida home	600,000
Artwork	100,000
Jewelry	20,000
Automobiles	35,000
Furniture	150,000
Cash value of life insurance	50,000
Value of your shares of the family business	5,000,000
TOTAL ASSETS	$7,580,000

Family Liabilities
(What you owe to others)

Mortgage on primary residence	$ 300,000
Home equity loan	50,000
Mortgage on Florida home	500,000
Automobile loans	10,000
TOTAL LIABILITIES	$ 860,000

Source: Ann M. Dugan

Once you have your snapshot, you can begin to analyze it. In the above sample, you see that:

—You have immediate access to $75,0000 cash.

—At some point in the past, your family lent $100,000 to the business or possibly your spouse did not take some paychecks because of business cash-flow issues. This is money that the business owes you and that should be repaid to you as business conditions allow. It is over and above whatever other ownership value your family has in the business. Think of it as a loan that was made and now needs to be repaid.

—You have stocks and bonds that, depending upon the transaction costs of selling them, could fairly quickly give you $300,000 in cash.

—You have access to pension and retirement funds of $650,000, but accessing that money may result in extra taxes or penalties.

—The cash value of your life insurance is $50,000.

—The latest valuation of the family business shows that your shares are worth $5 million. However, you can realize the cash only if the business is sold or your shares are redeemed. In many cases, a shareholders agreement spells out the conditions for the redemption of shares or for the sale of the business and how the cash from the sale is distributed.

—You own other things that have value but, in most cases, you must sell them to get the cash.

In looking at what you own and what you owe, it is important to determine the true value if you were to need cash for an emergency or major purchase, or if you simply need enough to pay monthly obligations. Consider:

—Your primary residence is worth approximately $500,000 if you sold it today. Your mortgage and home equity loan amount to about $350,000. Therefore, you would receive only $150,000 in cash from the sale less the real estate commission and closing costs. The true final amount of cash that you realize from the sale might be closer to $110,000-$115,000.

—If you sell your Florida home for $600,000, you would receive $100,000 cash less commission and closing fees.

—If you sell your cars, you would receive about $25,000 after you pay off your car loans.

The balance sheet also shows that your total assets exceed your liabilities by $6,720,000. While that's a good thing, remember that $5 million of those assets are tied up in the family business, and other funds, such as pension and 401k plans, may not be readily available.

Your own assets will differ from the sample balance sheet not only in dollars but in categories. Instead of artwork, you may have antiques or a valuable coin collection. You may have investments in properties that you rent out, or perhaps you have a substantial amount set aside in a college fund for the children. And, of course, your liabilities will be unique to you. Perhaps your house is paid off but you owe money on an expensive boat. Or perhaps your spouse borrowed money from his brother that needs to be repaid soon, or there's a buildup of credit card debt. You need to know these things.

2. The Family Income Statement. This statement shows, over a given period of time, the various ways that money comes into the household and how it is spent. Suppose your spouse, Sam, is the president of the family's business and receives a very comfortable salary and you do not work outside the home. Here is a sample of what your income statement might look like:

EXHIBIT 6

Family Income Statement

Family Sources of Income for Jan 1 through Dec. 31

Sam's salary from the family business	$550,000
Investment income	9,000
TOTAL ANNUAL FAMILY INCOME	$559,000

Expenses for Same Period

Mortgages	$ 40,000
Real estate taxes	20,000
Maintenance	20,000
Entertainment	12,000
Food	10,000
Travel	20,000
Automobiles (loans and use)	20,000
Insurance	18,000
Utilities	8,000
Clothing	25,000
Gifts and contributions	70,000
Income Taxes	200,000
Miscellaneous	50,000
TOTAL ANNUAL FAMILY EXPENSES	$513,000

Source: Ann M. Dugan

Because it is based on the income of the family and the way that money is spent, a Family Income Statement demonstrates what is required to maintain the family's current lifestyle without dipping into savings or adding to debt. In this example, the family brings in more money in a year than it spends and thus has the opportunity to direct its surplus of $46,000 into savings or other investments. The problem is that the family may have difficulty maintaining this lifestyle when the wage earner who is bringing in $550,000 a year from the family business can no longer do so.

Again, your own Family Income Statement will reflect your own situation and preferences. You may want to provide more detail, sorting out regular income from bonuses. If you are a working wife, you might want to show your income separately. If you or your spouse receives income from speaking engagements, you might have a separate category for honorariums. Your expenditures might look quite different. Suppose you support an elderly relative, or employ full-time household help, or are building a collection of rare books. The cost of any such items should be categorized under expenditures.

Like a household or business budget, a Family Income Statement makes an excellent planning tool. Suppose you and your husband have a set of twin girls and a boy all in high school. What will your income statement look like three years from now when all three are enrolled in college?

And what about retirement? Your balance sheet and income statements will help you decide together if you are setting enough aside for later years. You may even want to consider showing a separate section on bonuses and perks that the wage earner receives that will change or disappear on death or retirement. These can include such benefits as health and life insurance, use of a company car or airplane, club memberships, and resort vacations. How will their loss or reduction affect your lifestyle as a couple or the quality of life of the survivor after the death of a spouse?

What You Need To Know About Business Finances

Suppose you are a woman whose husband owns a business in its entirety or holds the majority of the stock in a company that was passed down to him and his siblings by their parents. And suppose you don't own any shares yourself and you don't work in the company. You've made a life of your own as a volunteer community leader and you have never really taken an interest in the afffars of the family business.

What you usually say when asked about the company is, "Well, that's my husband's business. I'm not involved."

The reality is that it isn't just your husband's business. It belongs to both of you. Your lives and your finances are intertwined. What happens in the business affects your quality of life for better or for worse. You may hope for its continued success so that it can be passed on to your children. Of course, there's the unfortunate possibility that your husband will die before you do, making it necessary for you to become involved in the business, perhaps even deciding to run it yourself (more on that later). These are perhaps the most important reasons for you to know as much as you can about family business finances.

But imagine that you are a 25-year-old single woman in a family that owns a plastic extrusion company that was started by your grandfather. You're working on a Ph.D. in history in hopes of teaching at the college level. You don't own any shares in the family business, although you know that within the next three years, your parents expect to start gifting small amounts of stock to you. "Why should I make the time and effort to learn about the business's finances?" you wonder. Your older cousins, Cliff and

Sandra, have been working in the business for many years and hold senior positions. In your eyes, it makes sense for them to be knowledgeable about the company's finances. You're happy to leave the finances to them. "The business is in Uncle Bradley's capable hands and doing well," you tell yourself. "And I have confidence that when Cliff becomes CEO, he's going to do a great job. Getting dividends will be an added benefit to my life."

Like some other young women who are future shareholders or small shareholders in successful, growing family firms, you may come to realize that your stake in the company will turn out to be your major source of income and wealth, far exceeding what most other occupations can provide. For this reason alone, you should want to learn to be an effective shareholder so that you can monitor your investment and contribute to the ongoing success of the company. And as for your cousin, Cliff, he will need the support and commitment of all the knowledgeable shareholders—and not just the males.

If you are a woman working in the company, you have probably already made it your business to learn as much as you can about its finances. In our view, however, women in business-owning families, whatever their involvement, need to educate themselves more about the business's finances than they often do. Unfortunately, we've seen too many women who own substantial stakes in their family companies but who leave the fate of their wealth to others because they resist learning about the companies' finances. Even if you are not working in the company or if you are not a shareholder yourself but are married to one, you owe it to yourself to become educated about the company. What happens to it affects your life.

What should you know about your family businesses finances? Here are the basics:

1. You should understand the business' financial statements—the annual report, balance sheet, income statement (also called the profit and loss statement, or P&L) and the cash-flow statement. This will help enhance your understanding of how the business is performing, and what variances exist between projected and actual performance. In addition, a five-year balance sheet and income statement will offer comparisons that help you see company performance over time, not just a snapshot at a given time. Knowledge of the financial statements will help you understand how well the business is doing, what the trends are, and where assets are.

A good place to start educating yourself is a book by our colleague, Norbert E. Schwarz, *Family Business by the Numbers: How Financial Statements Impact Your Business* (Family Enterprise Publishers®, 2004). You'll find more information on it in the Resources section at the end of this chapter.

2. You should be knowledgeable about any personal guarantees in the business that have been signed by your husband or by both of you. Often when a family business borrows money, the lender wants the signatures of the husband and wife as a personal guarantee that the loan will be paid out of the family's personal funds if the business itself cannot repay the loan. If

any personal guarantees have been made by you as a couple or by your husband, you'll want to understand what your liability or responsibility is.

3. It's important to know how the assets in the business are owned. When a business starts out, this is usually reasonably simple. There may be a single owner, or a husband and wife may own the business jointly. Or, it might be owned by two or three siblings or cousins.

As time goes by and a family business becomes older and larger, the ownership of assets can become very complicated. For example, the original business, a manufacturing company, might now be owned by your spouse but the real estate that the business sits on might be owned by another corporation that belongs to your retired father-in-law and his two brothers. Your spouse's sister might own a company, originally financed by your father-in-law, that leases equipment to your spouse's business as well as to companies outside the family. What is perceived as one business might in fact be many businesses—a manufacturing plant, a trucking company, a warehouse, all sitting on one piece of land. Sometimes what was thought of as a subsidiary becomes larger than the core business and unintended imbalances occur. If the leasing company outgrows your spouse's business, your sister-in-law may experience greater financial success. Or, perhaps the leasing business, for one reason or another, was set up so that your sister-in-law was majority owner and your husband had a small stake and everyone seemed to think he had a much larger share.

These kinds of things happen all the time. Consider franchises. In car dealerships, sports franchises and other such businesses, the franchise agreements typically require that there is a majority owner. Such requirements enable the franchisor to deal with only one owner at any given franchise. But suppose Dad, a widower who owns a sports franchise, dies, and his five children think they're going to each inherit 20 percent of the business. Instead, they gather at the attorney's office in a state of grief and learn that, according to the franchise contract, one of them must own at least 60 percent and four of them must divide the remaining 40 percent. Why didn't Dad ever tell them?

As the years go by, business owners sometimes actually forget how things were set up. It makes sense for business families to review how assets are held on a regular basis and to make the information clear to family members. If this isn't being done in your family, ask that it be done. Clarity about assets reduces confusion. It prevents shock, such as that which occurred when the five siblings learned that four of them would have to share 40 percent of their father's franchise, or when one's husband dies and she finds out that her husband's holdings in the family business were not as substantial as she expected. When family members understand how assets are held and why things were set up as they are, there's likely to be less bitterness when imbalances occur and, possibly, a greater opportunity to correct the imbalances.

Chapter VI

What Else Should You Know?

Some matters cut across both the business and the family. Two major plans that a wife should know about are the estate plan and the business succession plan. Ideally, if you are a wife, you should participate in estate planning. Such plans stipulate what will happen with all the assets of the domestic unit when one of the partners dies.

If you play a major, active role in the business, you might also contribute to succession planning. If you are not actively involved, you at least need to understand what the plan is (it may involve your children, after all). Basically, you will want to know such things as: How will the successor development and selection process work? Is this an ownership succession, a management succession, or both? And what is the difference between one type of succession and the other? How and when will stock be passed on to the successor(s)? Who, if anyone, will have majority control?

You should also understand key documents and know where they are kept. Below is a checklist of documents you should know about. This is not an all-inclusive list, as each family's situation is unique, but it does cover the basics:

EXHIBIT 7

Key Documents Checklist	Location of Document	Who To Call
_____ Shareholder or buy-sell agreements		
_____ Partnership or management agreements		
_____ Wills		
_____ Living wills		
_____ Power of attorney arrangements		
_____ Executor arrangements		
_____ Business valuations		
_____ Stock certificates		
_____ Trust documents		
_____ Estate plans		
_____ Personal tax returns from the last 2-5 years		
_____ Corporate tax returns from the last 3-5 years		
_____ Life, disability, long-term care, and other types of insurance documents		
_____ Investment portfolios		
_____ Real estate documents (mortgages, deeds, etc.)		

Source: Ann M. Dugan

Couples should review contracts and other key documents at least yearly and make necessary updates. If you're going through the process for the first time, don't be afraid to raise questions. Suppose you ask why you and your spouse don't have long-term care insurance and he says, "We really don't need it because we have cash flow from our stocks and bonds." Pursue the matter by asking for an explanation of the cash flow from those stocks and bonds.

It's helpful to think of you and your family as a small enterprise that must be run like a business. Know what your balance sheet is, where its income comes from, what are its expenses, what its obligations are, and where all its important documents are and what they mean.

What Should a Widow Do?

If you become widowed, should you keep or sell a business that was owned and run by your late husband? The answer to that question is "It depends." It depends in part on the structure and needs of the remaining family. Are there dependent children? Are older children already in the business or interested in making a career of the business?

It also depends on how interested you are in the dynamics of running a business, on the skills you can bring to it, and on your health, energy and financial situation. Further, it depends on the financial condition of the business itself. Decisions should be made only after a period of intense information gathering that includes discussions with professional advisors (accountant, banker, lawyer), the senior managers of the company, and trusted friends and associates, as well as the observations you make and the "gut feelings" you gain through spending time at the business. Consider this case, based on a true story:

> One beautiful September afternoon, Anita got the call that had been her greatest fear. Michael, her husband of 25 years, had had a heart attack at one of their restaurants and died en route to the hospital. Anita and Michael had been high school sweethearts and married right after graduation. With the financial help of Michael's parents, they soon opened a small restaurant. Anita worked there briefly before their first child was born. In the subsequent years, two more children arrived as did four more restaurants.
>
> Anita had begun to worry about Michael long ago. Over the years, he had put on many extra pounds. He worked very long hours, rarely exercising or taking time to relax. "Michael," she had often warned, "you're a heart attack waiting to happen." Unfortunately, her prediction came true. Now she had to decide what to do about the business.
>
> The restaurants were closed the day of Michael's funeral but Anita and everyone in the company knew they had to

reopen fast so that employees and customers would not disappear. After the services, Anita met with the restaurants' five managers to decide how to proceed, all agreeing that it was important to reopen the next day. During the meeting, one of the managers gave Anita some unpleasant news: the company was suffering from poor cash flow. According to stories her husband had told her while he was still alive, Anita knew he had thought three of his managers were very good but that he lacked confidence in the other two. Now she learned that two of the restaurants had experienced a decline in customer traffic as a result of new competition but had not adjusted their expenses and the three more profitable restaurants had to help them. The result was a company-wide cash shortage that Michael had tried to fix by borrowing short-term money from the bank while he figured out what to do. Anita was surprised to learn about the bank loan, too. Michael, she thought, was probably trying to protect her by not telling her about it.

Anita met with an uncle whose advice she valued and with some friends from church. They all believed that the restaurants were a great business and should be a good source of income for Anita. They all were sure that Michael would never want her to sell. Besides, there were five managers who actually operated the restaurants day to day, so there was not much Anita had to do but oversee things.

Ed, the business's outside accountant, was not so positive. He told Anita that the market was changing and that he had advised Michael for some time to put the restaurants up for sale. But Michael was emotionally tied to the business. Running it was all he had ever done and he could not be persuaded to act. Ed was also worried about an increase in employee theft, especially now that Michael's watchful eye was no longer there.

"Then there's the business cycle," Ed said. "I would encourage you to think about selling this fall. After the holiday season in December, the restaurant business slows down considerably until March or April. That always put a huge strain on cash flow and Michael would take on more work then to keep labor costs at a minimum. You'll have an easier time selling now and you'll get a better price."

Mourning the loss of her husband and confused by conflicting advice, Anita still had to make a decision. What would you do in her place? Here's the rest of the story:

Anita honored Michael's commitment to the restaurants and kept them open. Cash flow continued to decline and a detective that Anita hired caught one of the managers and several employees stealing cash, liquor, and food. Morale dropped throughout the restaurants because Anita's style of managing was much more authoritarian than Michael's and she wanted more control over what staff did during the day.

The holiday season was not as busy as it should have been and customer counts were way off. By March of the following year, cash flow had deteriorated to the point that Anita was considering closing several of the locations during the week and opening only on weekends. In May, her accountant introduced her to a potential buyer, who offered her 35 per cent of the valuation that she had been given in October during the settlement of the estate. After much consideration and many discussions, Anita decided to sell. She feared the continual erosion of the restaurants and she regretted not having sold at the top in the fall instead of during a slide toward the bottom in May. It was an emotional ride that could have been easier.

Does Anita's story mean that it's best to sell? Not at all. Other widows, including many without business experience, have chosen to run the family company themselves and have done so with considerable success. One such woman is Georgia Berner, who picked up the reins of her husband's company, Berner International Corporation, after he died in a small-plane crash in 1984. Originally founded by her husband's father, the New Castle, Pennsylvania, company manufactures equipment, such as air doors and air curtains, for retaining cool air indoors and keeping heat out, or vice versa.

Berner was a 42-year-old mother of four school-age children when she took over the company. She had been an English teacher and a leader in community organizations, but she had neither business nor engineering skills.

"I did not know finance at all, particularly its language," she once recalled. "During my first meeting with the bankers and accountants, I said, 'I don't have the faintest idea of what you just said!' But one of my strengths is that I am a questioner; I'm naturally curious, so I always ask questions. In fact, I still ask them!"[6]

She shored up her financial knowledge by attending a one-day course on cash flow sponsored by the U.S. Small Business Administration. She learned at meetings of her trade association, and she read copiously—business magazines, books on management, and newspapers and trade journals. Her CPA firm also gave her a crash course on accounting basics.

She recognized the company's need for marketing, and she was good at it. She also emphasized a business philosophy of providing the best possible product performance at the best possible price for the market.

Why did she decide to run the company instead of selling it or hiring someone else? She says her husband frequently told her that she would be better at the job than he was. "If anything ever happens to me, you run it," he said.[7]

She more than lived up to his faith in her. Under her leadership, company sales have grown by more than 600 percent.

A famous example of a widow who decided against many odds to run the company herself is of course the late Katharine Graham of the Washington Post Company. Her father had bypassed her and handed control of the company to her husband, Phil until his death in 1963. Despite receiving offers to buy the company and despite feeling terrified, Katharine Graham announced that she would run it herself. Her reason: she wanted to keep *The Washington Post* in the family. A self-described "doormat wife," Graham knew nothing about business. "The mere mention of terms like 'liquidity' made my eyes glaze over,'" she said.[8] But she educated herself and reinvented herself, becoming one of the most successful CEOs in the news business in the last century.

If a business-owning husband dies before his wife does, she's going to have to deal with that business in some way. Unless recently done, a business valuation will likely need to be performed to establish the fair market value for tax purposes and for a possible sale of the business. (As a starting point, talk to your accountant.) The business will need to be kept running until the wife decides to hire someone to run it, run it herself, or sell it. It's a good idea to have these discussions as part of the regular communication about the business. Then an interim plan can be put into place for keeping the company going until final decisions are made. You might want to read Craig Aronoff's article in the April 2002 issue of *The Family Business Advisor*® titled "Pre-Mortem Beats Post-Mortem."

Widows often know more than they think they know about running the business and are, in fact, semi-prepared to step in. They know the customers, they know the employees, and they know the products or services. In making a decision whether or not to run the business herself, a woman will often do a self-assessment. One long-time school teacher, faced with her husband's impending death from cancer, asked herself what skills she had that she could bring to his concrete company. She realized that her strengths included teaching and motivational skills, problem-solving ability, marketing and management skills, and a positive work ethic. All, she knew, were transferable to the concrete industry.

Don't Be Held Hostage by Advisors

New widows who have totally relied on their husbands to handle all the finances often find themselves at the mercy of their professional advisors—

attorneys, accountants, insurance agents, and the like. If the husband was in his later years, chances are the advisors were hired decades ago. Women frequently complain that advisors, particularly the older ones, are condescending. A husband may have said, "Listen, Joe's our accountant. He's been there forever. When I'm gone, he's going to take care of you and help you through all this." But what the wife finds is that Joe talks down to her or is intimidating, at a time when she is in mourning and is at her most vulnerable. Instead of being helpful, Joe tries to keep her even more clueless: "You've never touched a checkbook in 40 years of marriage. Why do you care now? You don't need to worry about this." Like some advisors, Joe is busy and doesn't get back to her promptly.

The best defense, of course, is to become knowledgeable about business and family finances long before a spouse dies or a divorce occurs. Make sure you are included in meetings with the advisors so that they know and respect you. If you lack such knowledge, when you meet with your advisors, ask each to be prepared to help you understand the status of the business and your personal situation. Gather all the information you need before you make any decisions. At the very least, deploy the 24-hour rule: all major decisions will get a minimum of 24 hours of contemplation and discussion.

The right emotional match with your professional advisors is crucial. If you do not feel that the professional is treating you appropriately or is not answering your questions in a way that you understand, find a new advisor. Likewise, if an advisor is pressuring you to take an action that you don't want to take ("Sell the business.""Sell the beach house."), don't be afraid to consult with a different advisor. He or she may offer an alternative that will enable you to do what you want to do.

Here are some questions a new widow should be asking her advisors:

Attorneys:

—How is the business structured and what is the effect of this structure on me and my family?

—What exposure to lawsuits does the business have?

—Explain the shareholder agreement.

—What is "power of attorney"? Basically, it's the legal right of one person to act on behalf of another, but ask your lawyer to provide details and find out who, if anyone, has power of attorney over you, the estate, or the business.

—What is the value of my estate?

—Is there an executor of the estate? Who? What rights and obligations does the executor have?

Accountants:

—What is the value of my estate?

—Explain the value of the family business and how the valuation was determined. Who determined it and when was this done?

—Is there life insurance or other provisions to cover taxes?

—Explain the buy-sell (shareholders) agreement.

—What will happen to the medical benefits that my children and I received through the family business?

—What opportunities will my young children have to be employed by the family business in the future? Will they own part of the business when they come of age?

—Should I pay off my mortgage now or wait? Why?

—Should I take income from our retirement plans?

—Should I sell or keep our vacation home?

Insurance Agents:

—What happens to the life insurance proceeds?

—What is second-to-die insurance?

—What happens to my life insurance contract now?

—What is the difference between the different kinds of life insurance?

—Should I have disability or long-term care insurance?

—What happens to the life insurance that the company has on my spouse?

—Should I have a life insurance trust?

Dealing with Reluctant Husbands

What if your husband is a man who likes to keep all the financial information to himself? You'll need some soft ways to start the conversations that will elicit the kinds of information you need to have. Here are some possible approaches:

1. Go back to the Key Documents Checklist on page 81 and give yourself a point for every document you understand and know where is kept. Then tally your grade:

0 to 3 = F (I'm totally in the dark.)

4 to 6 = D (I'm severely lacking in knowledge.)

7 to 10 = C (I have some knowledge but not nearly enough.)

11 to 13 = B (I have above-average knowledge but could benefit from more.)

14 to 16 = A (I'm extremely knowledgeable.)

Suppose you scored an 8. You might launch the conversation with your spouse by saying, "You know, I've just tested myself using this checklist. I only got a C. According to this book, I should really be working toward an A in understanding our financial picture but I need your help. Let's go over this list together so you can help me learn some of the things I need to know."

2. Encourage him to read this book or at least the parts that pertain to him. "Honey, there are some things in this book that we should be talking about. Let's take a look at it, especially the chapter on finances."

3. Offer to make some changes yourself. Maybe you can say something like, "You know what? I realize that I'm not being a very good role model to our children when it comes to money. Alyssa has gotten the idea that she won't have to worry about money because her father or a husband will take care of all that. Her brother already thinks that all the financial responsibility is going to fall on his shoulders when he's grown up and has a family. I don't think either of those ideas will be realistic when they're adults. I am going to more about the financial side of our lives so that I can set a better example for them. What do you think?"

4. Take advantage of an experience your friends may have had. "Linda told me she's been a wreck since Charlie died. He never told her anything about the financial side of his business or about their personal finances. Now she's having to deal with bankers and lawyers and accountants—you name it. She just learned that some of his life insurance is going to his ex-wife and the kids from the first marriage, and Linda's worried there won't be enough for herself and

One Widow's Assessment

So how did my education translate to the needs of an engineered product manufacturing business? Fine arts training gave me an eye for drawing; political science and social psychology (which is about demographics and "normal" behavior) gave me an understanding of people and hence of marketing; English literature gave me communication and articulation skills, plus a sense of breadth of the world in which we operate; the humanities taught me to question, to question and to question, to gather many sources, to be creative; raising children and living in Japan gave me organizational skills; history and the great works of literature throughout the ages taught me the importance of ethics and integrity in doing business.

Did I need a business degree to be successful? No, I did not. And when someone recently asked me that question, it led me to think that perhaps we would not have so many Enrons...in our current world if more people read about Ulysses and King Lear; read Faulkner and Winston Churchill, Emily Dickinson, Harriet Beecher Stowe, Ayn Rand; saw plays like "Cat on a Hot Tin Roof"—even "The Lion King"—because greed, treachery and false pride are as old as mankind, a tale told many times. And whether the tale is fiction or whether the tale is Enron, the plot never changes.

What my university education gave me was the tools for my mind—the ability to be resourceful, questioning, to express myself and to believe in myself.

—Georgia Berner
Excerpted from her address to graduates at Slippery Rock University, December 18, 2004.

her kids. There's talk that she'll have to sell the business. And she says the lawyer who Charlie promised would be so helpful just treats her like a child.

"Linda's problems made me realize that I don't know these things either. What if something happened to you? What can we do to make sure I know enough about our situation that I don't have to go through what Linda's going through?"

Starting difficult conversations with a resistant spouse may take courage. You may not have been brought up to talk about money, and he may think he'd be giving up power over this facet of life if he shares financial information with you. Be persistent and take advantage of events to re-introduce the topic when the opportunity arises.

What if you are not successful? You may never convince your partner to share information if he's from an extremely male-dominated culture or his age is such that he simply cannot change. One good strategy is to arm yourself with knowledge about business and about personal finance. Begin with some of the resources listed at the end of this chapter. In addition, take some courses. Adult night schools, community colleges, and various organizations often offer courses in personal and business finance. Once your spouse begins to realize how much you know in general, he may feel more confident about sharing the specifics of your family's situation with you.

If not, you'll still be ready to talk with those professional advisors if you find yourself on your own. And, unlike Katharine Graham, your eyes won't glaze over when someone mentions liquidity.

Resources

Books:

Family Business by the Numbers: How Financial Statements Impact Your Business, by Norbert E. Schwarz (Family Enterprise Publishers®, 2004). A practical guide to understanding the financial side of a family firm for individuals without a business background.

Family Finance: The Essential Guide for Parents, by Ann Douglas and Elizabeth Lewin (Dearborn Trade Publishing, 2001). Covers such topics as saving for your children's education, insurance, wills, and "raising money-smart kids."

How To Read a Financial Report: Wringing Vital Signs Out of the Numbers, by John A. Tracy (Sixth Edition, John Wiley & Sons, Inc. 2004). Teaches the basics of balance sheets, income statements, cash flow, and other financial measures and terms.

Making Change: A Woman's Guide to Designing Her Financial Future, by Neale S. Godfrey with Tad Richards (Fireside, 1997). An entertaining primer on money of particular value to younger women or to older women who lack experience in managing finances.

Money, a Memoir: Women, Emotions, and Cash, by Liz Perle (Henry Holt and Company, 2006). Helps women understand how emotions affect their relationship with money and suggests ways to break free of self-defeating attitudes and beliefs.

Preparing Your Family To Manage Wealth, by Roy O. Williams (Monterey Pacific Institute, 1992.) Focuses on creating healthy values and teaching children the responsibilities of wealth.

Women & Money: Owning the Power To Control Your Destiny, by Suze Orman (Spiegel & Grau, 2007). Offers a series of action plans for getting on top of one's finances.

The Stewardship of Private Wealth: Managing Personal & Family Assets, by Sally S. Kleberg (McGraw-Hill, 1997). Offers an education in such matters as money management, investment, philanthropy, and communicating about wealth.

Periodicals and Web Sites:

Money, a popular monthly magazine published by Time Inc. Emphasis is on personal finance.

The Wall Street Journal, the national business newspaper published six times a week by Dow Jones, Inc. (www.wsj.com). Of special interest are the sections called "Personal Journal" and "Money & Investing."

Worth, addresses issues confronting an affluent target audience. Published by CurtCo Publishing, LLC.

www.familymoneyconsultants.com. Click on "Publications" for online articles on such topics as prenuptial agreements, managing multi-generational money, the emotional meaning of money, and transferring assets to children.

Notes

1. Andriani, "Expense Account," p. 34.

2. Ibid.

3. Perle, *Money, A Memoir*, p. 227.

4. Ibid., p. 228.

5. Ibid., p. 229.

6. Sabol, "This Is Georgia Berner," June 2004. May 28, 2007, <http://news.pghtech.org/teq/ teqstory.cfm?id=1194>.

7. Lundstrom, "From Tragedy to Small-Biz Triumph," May 9, 2000. May 28, 2007, <http://www.businessweek.com/print/smallbiz/content/may2000/ma000509.htm?chan=sb>.

8. Graham, K., *Personal History*, p. 343.

VII.
Working with "Outsiders"

Intelligence is knowing what you don't know.
Wisdom is knowing who to ask.
Success is the courage to do so.
—A family business owner
[How To Choose & Use Advisors, p. 45]

Well, I don't know as I want a lawyer to tell me what I cannot do.
I hire him to tell me how to do what I want to do.
—John Pierpont Morgan, American financier
[Quotable Business, p. 214]

By "outsider," we mean any non-family individual who is in a position to interact with a woman in a business-owning family, whatever her role. Outsiders could be key non-family executives or independent members of the board. They might be vendors or clients. Typically, they are professional advisors, such as an attorney, a banker, an accountant, or a family business consultant.

Women in family firms generally have one of two things to say about outsiders, especially advisors:

1. They can be treasured allies. Or,

2. They can treat you like a child, trying to intimidate you or trying to get you to do what *they* want you to do rather than what *you* to do.

If you are an outsider, it's important to understand the benefits that accrue to you if women in family businesses see you as an ally, as well as to be aware of the risks you take when you approach them in an intimidating, authoritarian manner. Women family members working in the business increasingly have the power to hire, promote, or fire, or to determine what law firm, bank or accountant to use. If they don't have direct power, they still may impact these decisions. Even women family members not in the business may wield a great deal of influence. Lance Primis, the former non-family president of The New York Times Company, learned the hard way. He alienated both the male and female members of the controlling family, the Sulzbergers, treating all but Arthur Ochs "Punch" Sulzberger, the chairman and CEO, with condescension. Punch got wind of the family's unhappiness with Primis and listened to family members, including the women, not only those of his own generation but of the next generation as well. When he decided Primis had to go, Punch consulted his three co-owning sisters and won their backing. Primis was subsequently fired.[1]

If you are a male in a family business, particularly if you are the CEO, consider how your attitudes and behavior toward the women in your family and business can affect the way outsiders regard your wives, daughters, sisters, nieces, and female cousins. If you are condescending, you may be sending a signal to advisors, non-family employees, and other outsiders that they also have permission to be demeaning to the women in your family. If you treat women with respect, you are setting an example to outsiders that respect toward all women is expected from them as well. Respect is not to be confused with mere politeness. Respect means including women in meetings, seriously listening to women's views, asking for their opinions and advice, sharing information with them, and treating them as your equal. If they work in the business, it also means making sure they are trained for and given responsibility, are expected to perform successfully, and are promoted accordingly—just like the men in your business.

Perhaps no one better exemplifies these principles of respect than the late Mohammed Abdullah Al Khonaini, founder of Al-Khonaini General Trading & Contracting Co. W.l.l., a diversified Kuwaiti family firm. His daughter, Mona Al Khonaini, succeeded him as head of the company and, in a letter to her siblings, she wrote:

> From the very beginning, my father asked me to accompany him to all meetings, conferences, exhibitions, and fairs, whether they were business, commercial or social. In all places, he put me in front of the guests or friends and introduced me as "Mona, my business partner" rather than "Mona, my eldest daughter." My father's deference and respect inspired in me a great desire to continue his dreams of establishing a well-recognized company and making them come true. Since the first day of my stepping into the business world, I found no difficulty in communicating or dealing with people. Wherever I went, whether it was government offices, banks, companies or clients, I found respect.[2]

In other words, Mona Al Khonaini's father paved the way for her to achieve success by demonstrating to others that she was his valued partner. She, in turn, used her talents to transform the family enterprise into his vision of a widely-recognized business. "Today," she wrote, "[Al Khonaini] is a leading company in the Kuwait business world, and one of the best known."[3] She and her six siblings are all shareholders in the company. Her three brothers and one of her three sisters are active in the business.

What Women Can Do

Georgia Berner, the widow who assumed leadership of Berner International, offers some interesting perspectives on women in family businesses and their advisors. If you have to take over a company quickly like she did, she says, you have three major allies. "One is the attorney, one is the CPA, and one is the banker. They are truly your three best friends. They can teach you amazing amounts of information. My three were so incredibly helpful and mentoring and generous. I think that's a good source of teaching and education right there." (If you find yourself in the position of having to take over and your company is very small and is still using a bookkeeper instead of a certified public accountant, she recommends shifting to a CPA at least for the transition period. CPAs have to pass rigorous exams and the knowledge they have can be invaluable.)

Did Berner ever encounter advisors who talked down to her? "They may have done that and I didn't get it. That's possible," she answers with a hearty laugh. "But I think Eleanor Roosevelt said it the best. She said, 'No one can make you feel inferior without your consent.' Well, I didn't consent."

Using humor helps in coping with advisors, Berner points out. At the end of her first meeting with her advisors, she told them, "I don't know what on earth you just talked about!" It was said tongue-in-cheek and she believes most people would be afraid to make such a statement, fearing it would cause advisors to look down on them.

"As far as I'm concerned, the advisors were the ones at fault because they weren't trying to speak my language," Berner explains. "If you're afraid to say, 'What are you talking about?,' then you're giving them permission to look down on you. I just never did that."

If an advisor you're working with needs to put you down, that says something about that individual, she points out. "The people that I've worked with are not people who have that need."

It's very easy to feel insecure when you don't understand something. To counter such feelings, equip yourself to participate in your discussions with advisors and other outsiders. For example, if you are meeting with an estate planner for the first time and you know nothing about the subject, telephone the advisor and say, "I want to be prepared for our meeting and I need to better educate myself on this. What materials can you send me or refer me to that will help me be better informed?" Another way to get ready is to ask the advisor for an agenda for the meeting in advance. With that in hand, you can prepare your questions about the items on the list.

If you feel you are being talked down to, find out if the outsider treats other family members the same way. In any case, let your family know you don't appreciate the way the outsider is treating you.

What Outsiders Can Do

Georgia Berner's comments hold the key to making the working relationship between an outsider and a woman in a family business an effective one: Approach the relationship from an educational orientation.

Suppose you are a financial advisor with a new client, a law librarian in her early thirties. She is a shareholder in her family's business and has come into considerable additional wealth as a result of her father's recent death. Let's say you advised her father for many years and you know a great deal about the family's business as well as the family's financial picture. Because you are her father's age, you might be tempted to treat her as a kid rather than the adult she is. Because you knew the way her father liked things to be done, you might be tempted to recommend she do things like her father did. You might also be inclined to tell her she needn't worry because you'll take care of things for her, just the way her dad wanted. You might also assume, rightly or wrongly, that she doesn't know much about money.

But somehow, your first meeting with her doesn't go well. She bristles when you say you'll take care of everything. She seems annoyed at how courteous and fatherly you are. She asks so many questions, and when you tell her she doesn't need to worry herself about this or that, she drums her fingers impatiently on the arm of her chair. You schedule a second meeting with her before she leaves but she calls later to cancel.

Because of the generational difference, it's probable that what you saw as being helpful and polite, she saw as being patronizing and condescending. You wanted to spare her the burden of your troubling to explain the stock market or issues of risk and liquidity to her. What you didn't know was that she thought you saw her as ill-informed or unable to learn.

This scenario could happen in a number of different settings involving outsiders and women in business-owning families—between an independent board member and a woman family board member, a banker and a new widow, a non-family executive and a woman family shareholder, a lender or a vendor and a new woman CEO. An older, non-family executive may find a younger female CEO's leadership style as troubling. She's not leading the way her father did. He was the charismatic power figure and people did what he said. His daughter seems "weak." She listens to so many people before she makes a decision. These relationships are more complicated when the outsider is male and from an older generation. But difficulties can still arise even when the outsider is of the same generation and gender as the woman in the family business.

Here are some ideas that will help a non-family player be more effective supporting a woman in family businesses:

—Don't make assumptions. Find out where she's at. She may be more knowledgeable than you think. If she's not, you can guide her to sources of information and help her grow. Instead of trying to take over, as the financial advisor did in the example above, you can ask such questions as, "Where are you in your understanding of this? How can we assist you in some of the more important decisions you have to make?" A tweak in language can make all the difference!

—Find out what she wants or help her articulate it. Don't impose on her what you want or what you think she ought to want or ought to do.

—Let her know what her options are as you see them and let her make the decisions. Don't offer to take care of things for her. If she's reluctant to be responsible for her own choices, help empower her with knowledge. Be a mentor.

—Be a partner in her success. This is not the "manage it *for* me" approach to financial advising, rather it is a "manage it *with* me" approach. This approach is characterized by collaboration, transparency and reliability. Being a partner involves expanding wisdom about choices and alternatives, asking questions and providing guidance through life's stages.

—Respect the business-owning family, including the women members. As the case of Lance Primis at The New York Times Company suggests, the women are often influential and powerful in ways that may not seem obvious. They are also sensitive to slights and to decisions that favor males in the family. In another case we know of, a lawyer's advice to concentrate ownership of a family business in the hands of a brother/CEO alienated him from his sisters. He long regretted following the recommendation of the lawyer, who was not tuned in to male-female issues and the emotional ramifications of such a decision. Even though the CEO may be signing the paycheck, an outsider in an advisory role will do well to serve the whole family, not just the CEO.

—Avoid stereotyping—and watch your language. The fact that many people in the news these days suffer from foot-in-mouth disease suggests how easy it is to slip into making offensive comments about specific groups. We have seen such slips by advisors and other outsiders—demeaning gays or women, for example, not only backfire against the individuals who made the remarks but also create ill feeling in the family if the comments are not challenged.

—Make sure you are understood. Clarity is your responsibility. As Georgia Berner said, when you are in an advisory position, it's up to you to speak the client's language.

EXHIBIT 8

Benchmarks of Excellence in Advisors

1. Maintains up-to-date technical knowledge and shows strong interest in and commitment to his or her field.

2. Communicates openly in clear, simple language, helping educate family members when appropriate.

3. Seeks to know the family and business in depth.

4. Understands how families work and how the family and the business relate to each other.

5. Gives advice and counsel that suit both the family and the business.

6. Initiates periodic meetings with the client for update and review.

7. Is resourceful on clients' behalf, spotting opportunities and sharing information and contacts.

8. Shows empathy, patience and trustworthiness.

9. Is willing to work with successor generations.

10. Raises questions about the future.

11. Promotes collaboration among advisors.

12. Gives honest advice, even when it may jeopardize the client relationship.

Source: Aronoff & Ward, *How to Choose and Use Advisors*, Family Enterprise Publishers®, 1994.

Expertise from outside the family is needed by any business-owning family and can be particularly valuable to women as a source of knowledge and mentoring. Non-family individuals who interact with the family in any professional capacity are wise to offer its women the same respect they offer to its men.

For their part, women in family firms will do well to make clear what they want from advisors and other non-family professionals. What's more, they need to be unafraid of asking questions. Outsiders have valuable knowledge, so soak it up.

Chapter VII

Resources

Publications:

How To Choose & Use Advisors: Getting the Best Professional Family Business Advice, by Craig E. Aronoff and John L. Ward (Family Enterprise Publishers®, 1994).

More Than Family: Non-Family Executives in the Family Business, by Craig E. Aronoff and John L. Ward (Family Enterprise Publishers®, 2000).

Working for a Family Business: A Non-Family Employee's Guide to Success, by Christopher J. Eckrich and Stephen L. McClure (Family Enterprise Publishers®, 2004).

Notes

1. Tifft and Jones, *The Trust,* pp. 742-755.

2. Kenyon-Rouvinez, Adler, Corbetta, and Cuneo, *Sharing Wisdom, Building Values,* p.58.

3. Ibid.

VIII.
Women, Communication, and Leadership

The leader makes the team. This is pre-eminently the leadership quality—the ability to organize all the forces there are in an enterprise and make them serve a common purpose.
—Mary Parker Follett,
early twentieth-century management visionary

The right to be heard does not automatically include the right to be taken seriously.
—Hubert Humphrey,
Former Vice President Of the United States

It has often been suggested in recent years that women have different styles of communication and leadership than men do. We should add that women in family businesses face communications and leadership challenges that are specific to them or that are confronted by members of both sexes but perhaps experienced more intensely by women.

Communications Challenges

In famililes and businesses, focused effort can both minimize communication problems and enhance communication as an effective tool for achieving family and business goals. For the sake of our discussion, we are considering two basic forms of communication: (1) human interaction (getting one's message across, listening, etc.) and (2) sharing information. Compared to the first form, sharing information is pretty simple, and we offer ideas for doing it later in this chapter.

As for the first challenge, human interaction, we often find that women in business-owning families have a harder time being heard. One reason is that dads communicate with sons about the business more readily, especially if the sons work in the business and daughters don't. Even when daughters do work in the business, fathers, perhaps instinctively, often feel they need to protect their daughters more than their sons. Such feelings might prompt them to share less information with daughters. It's also often a father's perception that daughters are more emotional, leading a father to think the less his daughters know, the better. "If I don't tell them," he reasons, "they can't get upset." He might also have the same attitude toward his wife and sisters.

A significant part of the communication gap in family businesses often has to do with the differences in how men and women express themselves. While popular linguists today understand these differences as feminine (indirect, conciliatory, facilitative) or masculine (competitive, direct, aggressive) speech styles—not necessarily aligned with only women or only men, we are familiar with several examples that illustrate how women leaders unconsciously fall captive to a feminine speech style in situations where an alternative may be more appropriate.

Maria, first-born daughter of the founder recently earned her MBA and joined the leadership team of a manufacturing company. While her understanding of systems and processes in the classroom and outside work experience far exceeds that of the senior managers, she has a hard time convincing them to readdress some inventory issues. Driven by her desire not to condescend, and by cultural mores to be polite and pleasant, her speech pattern downplays her authority and assertion, and the suggestions fall on deaf ears.

Feminine style speech patterns tend to be less assertive and less intense, and the speaker, often modifies what she says, even in situations where her expertise is superior. She'll make a statement and include a hedge or softening phrase that weakens it, such as "sort of," "I guess," "give or take," or "kind of" not so much out of uncertainty, but as a way of mitigating the negativity, preserving collaboration or keeping a polite tone. As a result, Maria, like other women leaders in family businesses, may come across as less confident and perhaps even less believable than their male counterparts, when her intention was to be a team player, a contributor who does not offend or alienate.

Even on a more simple level, giving direction or orders get modified by the speech style the speaker uses. "Return the phone call today," is a directive using what is usually considered masculine style, while, "When you have a moment, would you mind returning the phone call for me, please," is commonly understood as feminine speech style.

Making oneself heard is not always easy, even when all hedges and softening phrases have been eliminated. In our previous example, if Maria had adopted a more masculine style, she likely would have been criticized as being too direct or aggressive. It's a tricky balance. Women in Maria's position are challenged to find a balance between speaking authoritatively without over-asserting—much like driving a car with a foot on the accelerator and a foot on the brake simultaneously. The best approach is to be aware of the style you are choosing and use it intentionally and strategically.

As we have pointed out in earlier chapters, there certainly are excellent family businesses where women do have a voice and hold CEO and other top leadership positions. Emily Heisley Stoeckel says, however, that being heard can take a very long time—especially when you're dealing with non-family colleagues. "It took years of their experience working with me and my learning to express my opinion before people could hear me," she says. Being a woman may have played a part in the time it took, but the fact that she was the founder's daughter and heir apparent and an owner to boot made things more difficult. Receptiveness to her ideas varied. Sometimes colleagues were very receptive. Other times they said, "That was a great idea," and gave credit to someone else.

But Heisley Stoeckel tells herself, "What is my ultimate objective here? Is my ultimate objective to get the credit or is it to be a leader in an organization that is making correct and successful decisions?" She opts for the latter. She believes being heard, at least by non-family employees, would also be difficult for a male family member in her position.

"In a family-owned business with professional management, you have to be better and you have to work harder than anybody else to earn the respect of those people, because they think that you're there only because you're family," she explains. "And so, it takes time. You can get a seat at the table but you don't necessarily get the respect. Without trust and respect, you don't get very far."

The surest way for a woman to gain a voice and be taken seriously is the same as it would be for anybody, male or female, family member or not: Equip yourself to fulfill your responsibilities. Put yourself in a position to earn the credibility and the respect that you need in order to encourage people to want to communicate with you. Women will be taken more seriously in family firms when the perception is that they are as credible as the men.

Watch your language. Are you hedging your statements in order to be polite, collaborative, well-received? Yes, there are speech strategies commonly associated with men and women, but effective communicators—male or female remain fluid in their ability to choose the appropriate strategy for a given circumstance.

If a business has not been open to women in the past and is welcoming women family members for the first time, some cultural changes may be in order to assure that adequate communication takes place. Brothers or male cousins in senior positions, for example, may have to make a deliberate effort to communicate the same information to sisters and female cousins in senior positions as they do to one another until doing so becomes entrenched. CEOs of male-dominated businesses may need to keep reminding senior managers, including non-family executives, that they are expected to communicate with female family employees just as they do with male family employees. Older executives not used to working with women may especially need such encouragement reinforced.

Women family members not employed in the business also have a "need to know." Many of the roles they play—such as shareholder, board member, or family council leader—require understanding of what is going on in a business, and we find that it increases women's comfort level when they feel they have sufficient information to participate and contribute. Information is essential to women even when they have more informal roles, such as when Mom serves as a mediator between two siblings working in the business or soothes the prickly relationship between her CEO husband and a son when they don't see eye-to-eye over the direction of the company.

Leadership Challenges

A woman family member who advances in a male-dominated business may find herself trying to emulate the leadership style that has permeated the company, possibly by being tough, authoritarian, decisive, and intimidating. As she sees it, this is the only way she can have her leadership be accepted and successful in the company—by being "one of the boys" and practicing a leadership style that is typically seen as masculine. She may also be adopting this approach because that's the way her CEO father or mother has been leading the company and it has gotten the company to where it is. Some questions to think about are: Is this approach comfortable or is it leading to ulcers? Is dad's leadership style appropriate for a new generation? Will siblings resist the attempt to lead like Dad? In many cases, the sibling generation must toss out the paternal or maternal leadership model and focus on a more involved, collaborative, team approach.

Sometimes parents and siblings get disturbed when a successor CEO, male or female, runs the company differently from the way Dad did. They may put pressure on the successor to go back to the old way of doing things. This can be hard on any successor but particularly hard if the successor is the first woman CEO of the company. She has even more to prove than a male successor.

Over the years, however, family business professionals have observed that each new stage of a business—founding generation, sibling generation, and cousin generation—requires different kinds of leadership, in response to different situations and circumstances.

Women leaders are generally perceived to be less authoritarian than male leaders—certainly those of the past—and more participative and concerned about relationship building. Do their styles truly result in greater productivity, as the Babson/MassMutual study suggests? We eagerly await further research.

Do women really communicate and lead differently from men? We think so. In our experience, women often communicate and lead in a preventive way. If they have even a sniff of potential conflict in a family firm, they'll jump on it before it turns into a full-blown problem. What we see men do, however, is react. If there's a hint of a problem, they often ignore it, either hoping it will get better or go away of that someone will come along and fix it. Women are more likely to step in and say, "Let's sit down and have a meeting about this," or, "Let's develop a policy so this doesn't happen again." Generally, women tend more than men to try to set up an infrastructure within a business to prevent conflicts from getting out of hand.

However, differences in communication style should not cripple people and keep them from understanding one another. Nor should one style of leadership be labeled good or bad. Under the right circumstances, any given approach may be effective. In their book, *Effective Leadership in the Family Business*, our colleagues, Craig E. Aronoff and Otis W. Baskin, describe four different styles of leadership—Directing, Coaching, Counseling, and Delegating. They posit that each is effective under certain conditions and suggest that leaders not adopt just one approach but learn to move back and fourth between styles as circumstances require.

Communication styles and leadership, however, are inextricably linked. The way an individual communicates bears greatly on whether or not that person's leadership will be accepted. A woman who aspires to leadership in the business or in the family might find it useful to attend communication or leadership training programs to find out how her communication style enhances or distracts from her ability to be accepted as a leader. Then, if needed, she can get some communication coaching to enhance her chance for leadership success.

What Families Can Do

From a communications standpoint, how can families prepare for the increased participation of women family members in the family business? How can communication support the assimilation of women into the family enterprise? The following ideas should be helpful:

—Create venues for communication and information sharing. These can include family councils, owners' councils, family meetings and retreats, newsletters, group e-mails, a family web site, telephone conferences, webinars and more. Make sure that the women in the family have the same access to these venues as the men do.

—Include communications training by professionals at family retreats or in the business. Such training helps people understand one another's styles and improve their own interpersonal communication. It can help individuals navigate the differences not only between the ways men and women communicate but between generations.

—Understand that actions really do speak louder than words. We saw, in Chapter VII, how Mona Al Khonaini's father took her with him to every meeting and respectfully introduced her as his partner. That action communicated her position much more effectively than if he had left her back at the office and simply told others that she was his partner. Families can be looking for actions that will communicate the message that women are valued in their own families and businesses and have equal opportunity if they show initiative and prepare themselves. If Dad takes a son to work with him on Saturdays, he should take his daughters, too. If inactive shareholders are sometimes permitted at board meetings, make sure the women are invited as often as the men.

In a similar fashion, families can support leadership development for daughters as well as sons. Here are some ways:

—Recognize that daughters and sisters—like sons or brothers—probably can't and shouldn't lead just as their parents did. Current leaders need to find the styles of leadership that are most effective to them and adapt them to meet the needs of the business in their generation, not the needs of the business in their predecessors' generation.

—Start helping girls build leadership skills when they're young. Teenagers can be given leadership assignments like planning activities and entertainment for younger children at a family reunion. Ask a computer-savvy high school or college student to organize a family committee to design the family Web site or teach computer skills at a family retreat. Encourage girls to participate in leadership programs in school and college.

—Again, the family can bring in professionals to conduct leadership training sessions at family meetings or within the business. An important aspect of such training might include additional aspects of communication, such as public speaking or making effective presentations.

—A career-development path can be laid out for a daughter to gain experience either in the business or the family. In the business, it might be aimed at preparing her for a senior-level executive position. In the family, her ultimate goal might be to chair the family council or owners council.

—The family or the business can send daughters as well as sons for training at an institution like the Center for Creative Leadership or to a program sponsored by a family business center, such as the Next Generation Leadership Institute at Loyola University Chicago. (See the Resources list below.)

What Women Can Do

Women, of course, can assume responsibility for themselves. They don't have to wait for their families or their businesses to offer opportunities. They can take the initiative and sign up for seminars or courses that will enable them to improve their communication and leadership skills. They can read books and publications. They can go on the Internet for more information. The Resources list offers a good start.

Chapter VIII

Resources

Books and Publications:

Conflict and Communication in the Family Business, by Joseph H. Astrachan and Kristi S. McMillan (Family Enterprise Publishers®, 2003).

Effective Leadership in the Family Business, by Craig E. Aronoff and Otis W. Baskin (Family Enterprise Publishers®, 2005).

Many books by linguist Deborah Tannen can be helpful in workplace and family communication. Among them are: *You're Wearing That? Understanding Mothers and Daughters in Conversation* (Random House, 2006); *Talking from 9 to 5: Women and Men at Work* (Quill paperback, 2001); and *You Just Don't Understand: Women and Men in Conversation* (Quill paperback, 2001).

Leadership Education:

Babson College Center for Women's Leadership, Babson Park, Massachusetts 02457-0310; (781) 239-5001 or http://www3.babson.edu/CWL.

Center for Creative Leadership, One Leadership Place, P. O. Box 26300, Greensboro, North Carolina 27438-6300; (336) 545-2810 or http://www.ccl.org. CCL offers programs in North America, Europe and Asia, including a course geared toward women.

Leader to Leader Institute, 320 Park Avenue, 3rd Floor, New York, New York 10022; (212) 224-1174 or http://www.leadertoleader.org. Aimed at social sector leadership but programs and the Web site are applicable to other fields. Founded by management legend Peter F. Drucker.

Next Generation Leadership Institute, Loyola University Chicago Family Business Center, 820 N. Michigan Avenue, Suite 314, Chicago, Illinois 60611; (312) 915-6490 or http://www.sba.luc.edu/familybusiness.

IX.
Choices and Challenges

We started this book with the slogan, "Girls can do anything." We're closing with the notion that "Family businesses can do anything." We believe both to be true. In this age of information and technology, more than ever, girls can do anything. We'll grant that women's physical strength is generally not the same as that of men, but we now know that women can be successful as police officers, air force pilots, fire fighters, and telephone linemen. We also know that they can succeed at being heads of state, CEOs, CFOs, entrepreneurs, department heads, CPAs, and a host of other jobs that rely not on the ability to lift 50 pounds but on brainpower, character, leadership, and personality.

But family businesses also can do anything, depending on what they choose. Because family businesses do have a choice. They can follow tradition or they can break the mold and venture into a new realm of opportunity by drawing on the talents of their virtually untapped resources—women.

We feel somewhat like the after-dinner speaker who gets up before an audience and crumples up a prepared speech in favor of something off-the cuff but far more relevant. We had a lot of things we wanted to tell you but, well, something more crucial came up.

Initially, we were going to remind business-owning families of a number of important things, and here they are:

—Be gender neutral. Take girls to the office/plant/warehouse just as you would the boys in the family. Have them sweep the floor and stock the shelves. Imbue them with love for the business.

—Make it known that your family and your company believe in equal opportunity. Develop a family employment policy that is, again, gender neutral.

—Be mentors to young women as well as young men. Even better, make sure that your company and family have women who can serve as mentors.

—Help girls think about their future. Help them understand that they can do anything, as long as they have the talent and develop it. And help them develop it.

—Re-think your daughters-in-law. Some business-owning families cherish them and give them a chance to shine. Others fear and distrust them and worry about what will happen if there is a divorce. Fear or embrace sons-in-law and daughters-in-law on an equal-opportunity basis. Hopefully, you can embrace both. As you have seen, we were struck by the daughters-in-law who not only held family businesses together for the next generation but who, through their imagination and leadership, substantially enhanced the businesses and families into which they married. We are thinking of Georgia Berner, Evelyn Lauder, Amalia Lacroze de Fortabat, Ronda Brubacher, Yvonne Edmond Foinant, Ardath Rodale, and countless others.

—Make it clear to the males in the family, especially the next-generation males, that the females have equal opportunity. This doesn't require lecturing. Simply provide equal education, equal early learning experiences, equal exposure to the business, and equal participation in it. Set the expectation that everyone, regardless of birth order or gender, has an opportunity. Make it clear that the best person for the job will be selected for that job. Encourage teamwork—maybe even shared leadership if the kids work well together.

—Equip daughters as well as sons with good financial education. Don't imbue daughters with the idea that someone else will "take care of them." Enable them to take care of themselves. That's the best defense against their marrying gold diggers, and it holds true for sons as well.

—Send the message to key non-family executives, advisors, clients, and vendors that the women in your family have equal status with men. Enforce the message.

—Respect the need for work/life balance, not just for your daughters but also for your sons. It shouldn't be a "woman's" issue because it's a human issue.

—Don't despair if your daughter wants to do something other than join the family business when she's young. Leave the door open. Consider Miuccia Prada, who first shunned her family's luxury goods product company in Italy but who later became its leader of innovation.

—Also don't despair if a daughter decides to raise her children before joining your company. If she puts time aside to be a mother, remember that she's not only raising the future generation of family business leadership but she's also sacrificing an opportunity to build her own career until a later date.

—Don't let a daughter or any family member abuse their position if they are in the business. We have seen soft parents hire daughters—and sons—when there were actually no positions available that matched their education or skills or desires. We have seen the same sons and daughters sit at their computers on office hours, doing nothing constructive for the business but spending a lot of time and money shopping on the Internet.

To women in business-owning families, before we threw our speech away, we would have said:

—Be an advocate for yourself. You don't have to be pushy about it, but make your aspirations known and invite your family to help you get where you want to go—in the business itself or in family leadership.

—Prepare, prepare, prepare. There are so many significant roles you can play. Select those that appeal to you and make yourself ready to do a good job.

—Gird your loins, particularly if you desire to rise in the business. If you have siblings and particularly if you have brothers, you may have to fight hard to attain your goal—especially if it's a top leadership role. This may also mean sacrificing family harmony if your brothers' expectations are that males should lead the company and have favored ownership positions.

—Resist the temptation to take advantage of family connections if you work in the business. To earn credibility among non-family employees, you will probably have to work harder and longer than anyone else. Beginning your career elsewhere will allow you to learn and make necessary mistakes before joining the family business.

OK. These were the highlights of the speech that got thrown away. Don't ignore them. They're important.

What we decided to look at instead, however, are the decisions that a forward-looking business-owning family must deal with once it begins to entertain the notion that women truly are essential to the business's success. Let's look first at some of the old ways of thinking about women in family business and the new ways of thinking that could be possible:

EXHIBIT 9 ▰▰▰▰▰▰▰▰▰▰▰▰▰▰▰▰

Ways of Looking at Gender in Family Business

Old:

Only a son (preferably the first-born) can be the leadership successor.

New:

The most able person, regardless of gender or birth order, will be the leadership successor. If there's no able leadership within the family, we will go outside the family.

Old:

Only male family members are permitted to join the family business.

New:

Any talented family member may join the business provided there is a suitable opening and the applicant meets the criteria set forth in our family employment policy.

Old:

Female family members can join the family business only if they are willing to play supportive, often invisible roles.

New:
Family employees and non-family employees, regardless of gender, have the opportunity to advance in accordance with their ability.

Old:
This is a man's business. They'd make mincemeat of my daughter in this industry.

New:
Women have run or are running truck fleets, meat-packing plants and construction companies. Why not my daughter?

Old:
Women should be home taking care of the kids.

New:
Our daughters are so talented—they've figured out how to get the kids taken care of and work outside the home, too. Today, men and women partner in childraising. Our business is lucky to have them.

Old:
Our daughter stayed home and raised three children. Now she wants to join the company, but she's inexperienced in this business and she hasn't paid her dues.

New:
Our daughter is only 43—she could be working here a long time. She got great experience volunteering year after year and being a United Way officer. We think she's paid her dues—she raised some of the next generation's leaders. Let's give her a chance.

The reason we threw away our first "speech" is that, as important as the issues it raises are, it is not as forward-thinking as our "new speech." And our new speech isn't a speech at all. It's just a series of questions, very important questions. These questions assume that your business-owning family is open to the emergence of women in leadership positions in the family or the business itself. We must also say that these questions reflect our own excitement about the future of family businesses as they embrace the possibility of assimilating women into business and family leadership.

Here are the questions our "new speech" puts forth. And they are questions you must answer for your business and your family:

1. If our family welcomes the involvement of daughters on a level equal to sons in the business, how will that affect family harmony? Are our sons still expecting to benefit from traditional male biases?

2. Can we and will we raise sons who are comfortable with the idea of their sister leading the company or assuming other leadership roles?

3. Can we give other roles in our family business the recognition and rewards that they deserve—such as mother, family leader, foundation leader, and so forth?

4. Do we understand that our daughter is no less committed to the business than our son, even though she has taken time out for having children? Do we understand that women, of necessity, often have "non-linear" careers, as opposed to our sons, who join our business at entry level and proceed from there nonstop as from A to Z?

5. Do we see that human longevity might offer some advantages in our family business that we hadn't seen before? Maybe now our daughter can join at a later age and learn the ropes while her still-healthy father is available to offer guidance and make decisions while she learns.

6. Can our daughters act as advocates for themselves, or do we need to provide a boost? Research tells us that girls are more likely to be quieter about their opinions and their knowledge. Are we willing to investigate what we can do to help them blossom into leaders?

—Can our family overcome its prejudices and welcome the participation of 50 percent of its talent—the women? If not, what's holding us back?

These are obviously questions meant to stir your thinking, and certainly questions that might be discussed at a family meeting. On top of these, we have others to ask

How difficult is the challenge to assimilate women family members in a family business? One issue is the willingness of the women to push for participation. Another is the willingness of a male founder/CEO to see the women in his family as serious contributors to a business that he may view as "his." He may say and may genuinely feel that he created the business for his family, but passing on leadership and power and ownership to a daughter may not be exactly what he had in mind. Culture will play a very strong role. In most parts of the world and indeed, in many parts of the United States, male dominance prevails. The United States may be leading in its acceptance of women in significant roles in family businesses, but if your heritage is more strongly patriarchal, the family may still lean heavily toward males inheriting leadership and ownership of the family business.

Another factor is the entrepreneurial personality itself. Throughout most of history, businesses have been founded by men. Only in the last three decades have women begun to outpace men in starting businesses in the United States, which means men still own most of the businesses.

It takes a lot to measure up to and sometimes go against personalities as strong as entrepreneurial fathers—particularly if you are a daughter and your father, like any parent, is already a powerful figure in your life. It's hard enough for a son, even a favored son, under similar conditions. A comforting factor to consider though, is that according to our experience and some early research—a father/daughter succession is much less conflictual and much smoother than a father/son succession.

Birth order matters, too. Traditionally, businesses have gone to the first-born son. This is still true in many parts of the world. If businesses didn't go to the first-born son, they went to other sons. But what if there is a first-born son, or even other sons, and the daughter, a middle child, is the shiniest apple on the tree? It's a struggle for both the family as a whole and for the daughter in question, because the tradition of sons inheriting a business is still so entrenched.

So, family businesses face many questions they never had to answer before.

In our view, these are evocative questions. They are indicative not only of the choices that family businesses are facing but also of the freedom and power that they have to change the world. Will family businesses elect to follow the same old traditions, or will they burst out and open themselves up to new talents that can define their future—the women in their families?

We don't know the answer to that question or the others posed here. We only know how exciting the future can be, depending on the choices that business-owning families make.

Bibliography

Alderfer, Inc. "Our Company History." February 27, 2007. <http://www.alderfermeats.com/about/history.aspx>.

Allen, I. Elaine and Nan S. Langowitz. "Women in Family-Owned Businesses." Babson Park and Springfield, Massachusetts, Babson College/MassMutual Financial Group, August, 2003.

Andriani, Lynn. "Expense Account." *Publishers Weekly,* December 19, 2005, pp. 34-35.

Aronoff, Craig E. and Otis W. Baskin. *Effective Leadership in the Family Business*. Marietta, Georgia: Family Enterprise Publishers, 2005.

Aronoff, Craig E. and John L. Ward. *Family Business Ownership: How To Be an Effective Shareholder*. Marietta, Georgia: Family Enterprise Publishers, 2001.

—-. *How To Choose & Use Advisors: Getting the Best Professional Family Business Advice*. Marietta, Georgia: Family Enterprise Publishers, 1994.

"Balancing Work and Family in Family-Owned Businesses." Unpublished study sponsored by Loyola University Chicago Family Business Center and conducted by MK Consultants, Ltd., Evanston, Illinois, 2001.

Brubaker, Harold. "Acquisitions More Than Double Size of Alderfer." *The Philadelphia Inquirer*, August 23, 2004, pp. E1, E12.

Bundles, A'Lelia. *On Her Own Ground: The Life and Times of Madam C. J. Walker*. New York: Scribner, 2001.

Chemical Heritage Foundation. "Testing the Waters: Kathryn Hach-Darrow." May 28, 2007. <http://www.chemheritage.org/women_chemistry/health/darrow.html>.

Coutts & Co. *Coutts 2005 Family Business Survey*. London, 2005.

Danco, Katy. *From the Other Side of the Bed: A Woman Looks at Life in the Family Business.* Cleveland: The Center for Family Business, 1981.

Danco, Léon A. *Inside the Family Business*. Cleveland: The Center for Family Business, 1980.

The Estée Lauder Companies Inc. "Evelyn H. Lauder." March 22, 2007. <http://www.elcompanies.com/the_company/evelyn_h_lauder.asp>.

The Estée Lauder Companies Inc. "Heritage." March 22, 2007. <http://www.elcompanies.com/heritage.asp>.

Fearon, Francesca. "Obituary: Fiamma Ferragamo." *The (London) Independent*, October 6, 1998. March 16, 2007. <http://www.findarticles.com/ p/articles/mi_qn4158/is 19981006/ai_n14195534>.

Galloni, Alessandra. "The 50 Women to Watch 2005: The Owners: 2. Miuccia Prada." *The Wall Street Journal*, October 31, 2005, p. R11.

Gelles, Jeff. "Milsteins' Biggest Deal." *The Philadelphia Inquirer*, January 19, 2006, pp. C1, C8.

—-. "Twists, Quirks and Coats." *The Philadelphia Inquirer*, January 22, 2006, pp. E1, E4.

Graham, Donald E. "The Gray Lady's Virtue." *The Wall Street Journal*, April 23, 2007, p. A17.

Graham, Katharine. *Personal History*. New York, Alfred A. Knopf, 1997.

Hach Scientific Foundation. "About Hach Scientific Foundation: Deeply Devoted to Chemistry." 2005. February 27, 2007. <http://hachscientificfoundation.org/about.shtml>.

Hechinger, John. "The Tiger Roars." *The Wall Street Journal*, July 17, 2006, pp. B1, B4.

"The 100 Most Powerful Women: #65 Güler Sabanci." August 31, 2006. May 28, 2007. <http://www.forbes.com/ lists/2006/11/06women_Guler–Sabanci_E1WD.html>.

Israel, Lee. *Estée Lauder: Beyond the Magic*. New York: Macmillan Publishing Company, 1985.

Johnson Publishing Company. "Linda Johnson Rice." 2005. December 18, 2005. <http://johnsonpublishing.com/assembled/management_lindajrice.html>.

Karnitschnig, Matthew. "Sumner Redstone Settles Suit with Son over Family's Fortune." *The Wall Street Journal*, February 3-4, 2007, p. A2.

Kenyon-Rouvinez, Denise H., Gordon Adler, Guido Corbetta, and Gianfilippo Cuneo. *Sharing Wisdom, Building Values: Letters from Family Business Owners to Their Successors*. Marietta, Georgia: Family Enterprise Publishers, 2002.

Bibliography

Kroll, Luisa, and Allison Fass, editors. "Billionaires: The World's Richest People." *Forbes*, March 26, 2007, pp. 104-208.

Lauder, Estée. *Estée: A Success Story*. New York: Random House, 1985.

Longaberger, Dave. *Longaberger: An American Success Story.* New York, HarperBusiness, 2003.

Lundstrom, Meg. "From Tragedy to Small-Biz Triumph." Business Week Online, May 9, 2000. May 28, 2007, <http://www.businessweek.com/print/ smallbiz/content/ may2000/ma000509.htm?chan=sb>.

Malan, Allan and Deanna. "Mabel's Magic Mixes." *Michigan History Magazine*, January/February, 1998. January 2, 2007. <http://www.jiffymix. com/michhistory.htm>.

Maxwell, Kenneth, and Sofia Celeste. "New Blood at Ferragamo." *The Wall Street Journal*, October 10, 2006, p. B4.

Nelton, Sharon. "Leading the Family." *Family Business*, Autumn 2006, pp. 66-69.

—-. "Stepping Up." *Family Business,* Autumn 2005, pp. 43-46.

O'Hara, William T. *Centuries of Success: Lessons from the World's Most Enduring Family Businesses*. Avon, Massachusetts: Adams Media, 2004.

Perle, Liz. *Money, A Memoir: Women, Emotions, and Cash*. New York: Henry Holt and company, 2006.

Pirone, Jane. "Craigie Zildjian—CEO Avedis Zildjian." Drummergirl.com. February 18, 2004. April 11, 2005. <http://www.drummer girl.com/interviews/zildjian/ zildjian.htm>.

Powell's Books. "Emily Powell Will Lead Powell's Books into the Future. April 12, 2006. May 2, 2007. <http://www.powells.com/news_emilypowell .html>.

Rosen, Judith. Passing the Torch." *Publishers Weekly*, January 2, 2006, pp. 20-21.

Rubin, Nancy. *American Empress: The Life and Times of Marjorie Merriweather Post.* New York: Villard Books, 1995.

Sabol, Kristen. "This Is Georgia Berner." *TEQ Magazine*, June 2004. May 28, 2007, <http://news.pghtech.org/ teq/teqstory.cfm?id=1194>.

Salganicoff, Matilde. "Clarifying the Present and Creating Options for the Future." *Family Business Review,* Volume III, Number 2 (Summer 1990), pp. 121-124.

"Shoes: A Love Story, How Ferragamo's Widow Saved His Fashion Empire." October 10, 2006. March 16, 2007. <http://www.showbuzz.cbs news.com/stories/2006/10/10/ style_fashion/main2077547.shtml>.

Sims, Gayle Ronan. "Jeanne B. Fante, 96; Built Cookware Store." *The Philadelphia Inquirer,* June 23, 2006, p. B11.

Spragins, Ellyn, editor. *What I Know Now: Letters to My Younger Self.* New York: Broadway Books, 2006.

Tifft, Susan E. and Alex S. Jones. *The Patriarch: The Rise and Fall of the Bingham Dynasty.* New York: Summit Books, 1991.

—-. *The Trust: The Private and Powerful Family Behind The New York Times.* Boston: Little, Brown and Company, 1999.

United States Department of Labor. Bureau of Labor Statistics. "Women in the Labor Force: A Databook," 2006. Current Population Survey. May 27, 2007. <http://www.bls.gov/cps>. Path: Economic News Releases, Reports and Summaries, "Women in the Labor Force: A Databook," Table 25: "Wives who earn more than their husbands, 1987-2004."

"Use of Workplace Work-Life Benefits by Dual-Earner Couples." May 27, 2007, <http://www.princeton.edu>. Path: Family friendly programs.

Index

Index

Index

Chapter I